PUNK RESEARCH SERIES
Volume One

Theoretical Writings on Punk, Nation, State, Art,
Bureaucracy, and Socialism

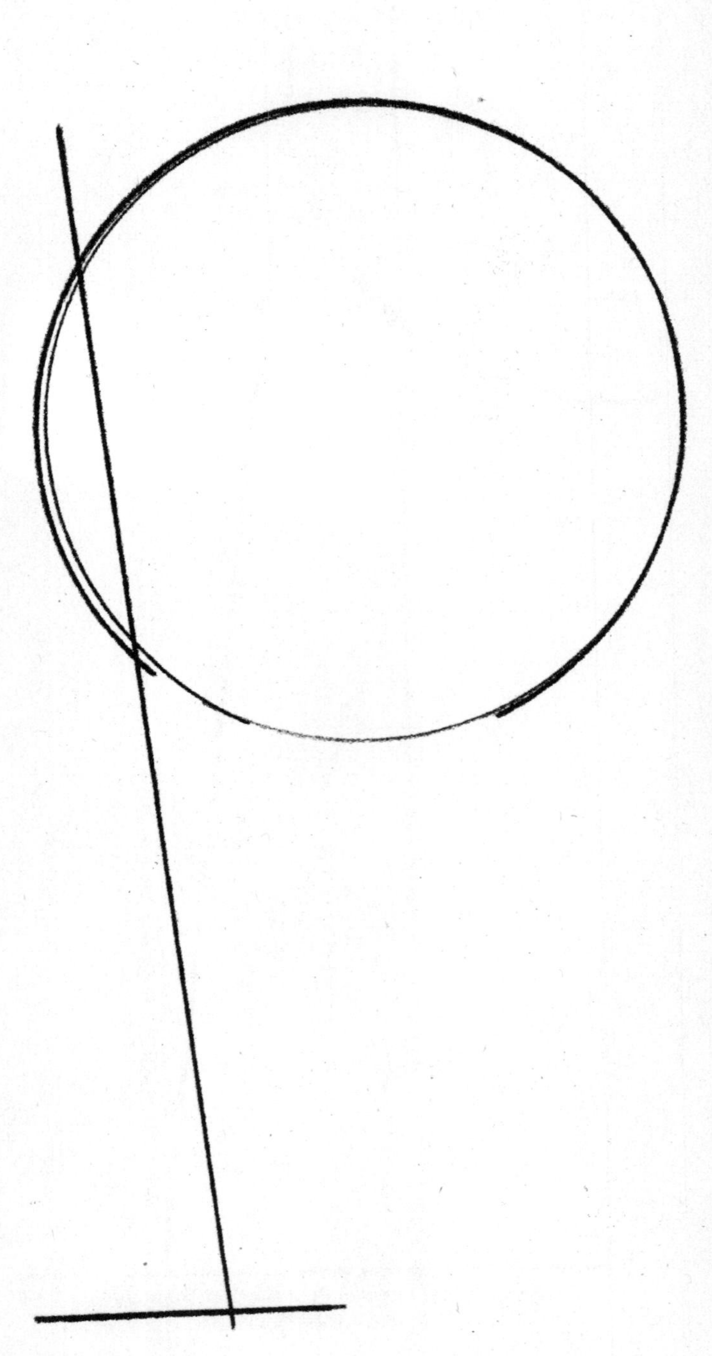

PUNK SUPREMATISM
Theoretical Writings on Punk, Nation, State,
Art, Bureaucracy, and Socialism

Translated by
Borut Praper, Dušan Grlja

Rab-Rab Press
Helsinki, 2025

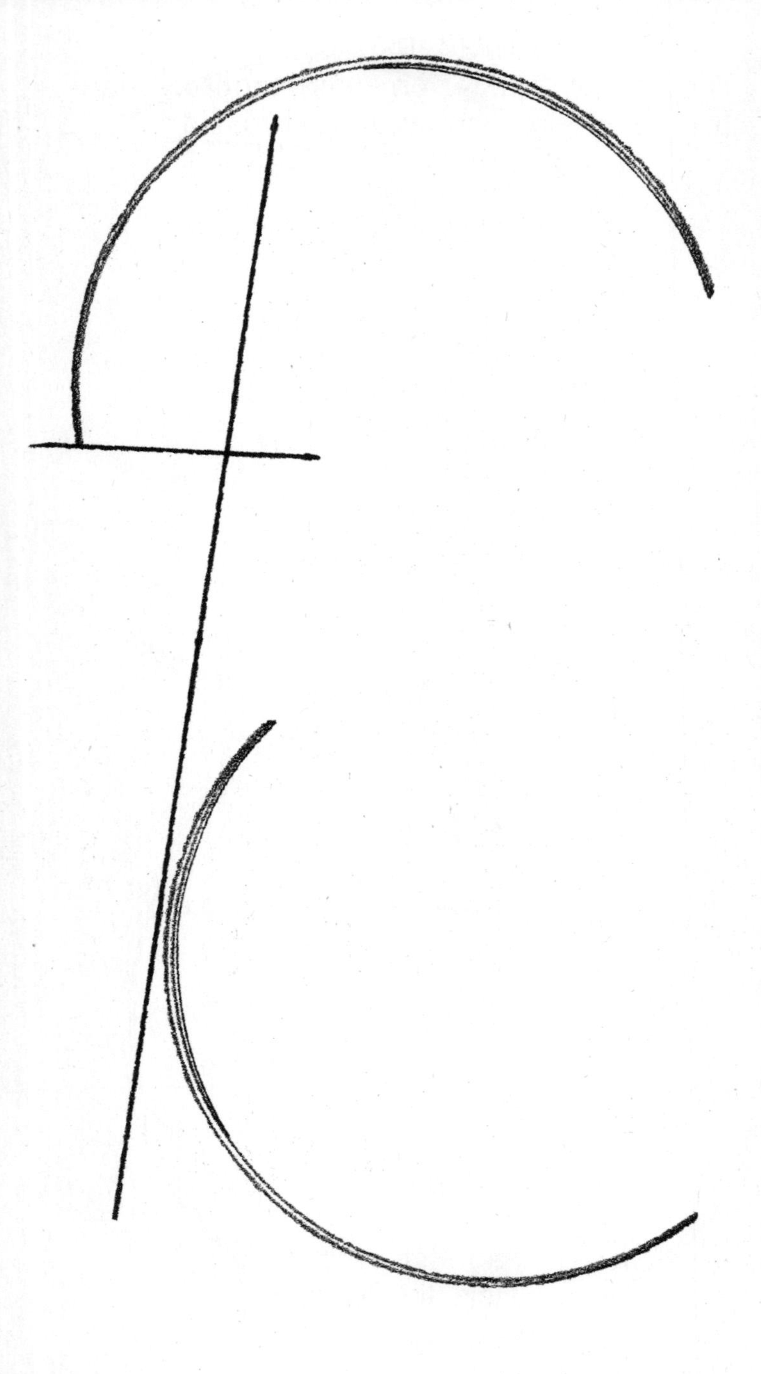

CONTENTS

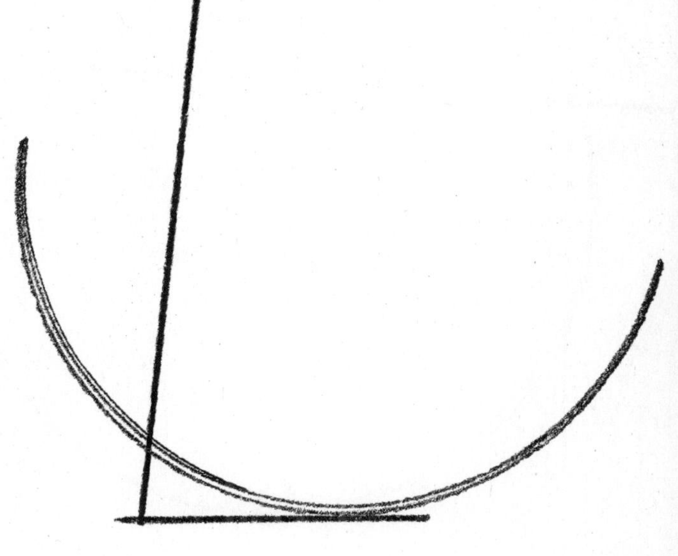

THE ADDITIONAL ELEMENT OF PUNK
Sezgin Boynik

Here are the first English translations of three theoretical texts published in Ljubljana, Yugoslavia, in the early 1980's. All three deal with ideology, nation, mass culture, and contemporary art, and are written under the influence of punk.

The opening text is by Rastko Močnik, a renowned philosopher and activist, whose contribution 'Reason Wins' [Razum Zmaguje] first appeared in *Punk Pod Slovenci* [Punk Under the Slovenes] in Ljubljana in 1985. Published in a run of three thousand copies by Knjižnica Revolucionarne Teorije [KRT, Library of Revolutionary Theory], *Punk Pod Slovenci* is a dense book of over five hundred pages. It is co-edited by Tomaž Mastnak, then a sociologist known best for his book dedicated to the critique of Stalinism, now a highly respected researcher on the early formation of European identity. The book includes articles, documents, interviews, transcripts, and statements related to the punk movement in the Socialist Republic of Slovenia, which was the subject of numerous public discussions and political platforms.

Močnik, who was commissioned to write 'Reason Wins', was a sociology professor in 1984 when he authored the text. He had already written numerous articles on literary theory, ideological formation, philosophy of Althusser, historical-materialist semiotics, and published theoretical commentaries about then pressing discussions in popular culture, education, and penal codes in the socialist state. The text on punk is one such theoretical intervention, commenting on the unprecedented ideological effect of punk mass culture.

Alongside Močnik is a text by Slavoj Žižek, whose writings are known to many English speaking readers, but whose intellectual and theoretical work during socialist Yugoslavia is still largely unknown. The text we publish here is not the only one Žižek wrote about punk. He has numerous texts discussing Laibach and the Neue Slowenische Kunst. Laibach was an industrial-punk band from Ljubljana belonging to art collective Neue Slowenische Kunst, whose work was the subject of many theoretical speculations.

Žižek's text published here is called 'A Few Thoughts About the Issue of the Ideological Presuppositions of Punk', and was originally published in the *Problemi* journal in 1984. The text itself was part of a larger research project on the formation of the identity of Slovenians, of which the early version was published with the same title in 1983 by the Institute of Sociology, focusing on the studies of self-management. This was Žižek's initial work dedicated to studying the "role of unconscious phantasms in the process of forming of identity", that culminated in his first English-language best-seller, *The Sublime Object of Ideology* (1989, Verso), carrying on even further the idea that Lacanian concepts could be the way to surpass the assumed misgivings of Marxist theoretical tools when dealing with profound ideological operations. Punk was the entry point to this new psycho-political domain. One of the earliest texts by Žižek on this subject, 'Ideology, Cynicism, Punk', was published in 1983 in a collection dedicated to philosophy through psychoanalysis.

'Ideological Presuppositions of Punk' was published in *Problemi*, one of the most progressive and avant-garde journals to exist during the period of socialist Yugoslavia. Močnik and Žižek served as its editors. It was a journal publishing concrete poetry (in 1968 and 1971, whole issues were published as special "artist-magazines" including nothing but experimental poems), politics, literature, and theoretical discussion (especially Lacanian and Althusserian theory, which became the hallmark of the Ljubljana School of Psychoanalysis). From 1981 to 1983, *Problemi* published three special issues under the alternative name *Punk Problemi*. The first *Punk Problemi* issue was published in 1981 (no. 205-206), and it introduces a very short theoretical framework for "punk-as-symptom", basing its position on the orthodox Freudianism influenced by Lacan, and aimed at reading the absent but fundamental features of society and ideology through punk. It is written by Žižek, then editor of *Problemi*. The remaining pages of that same issue are reserved for punk lyrics, images, statements, etc., in other words, as the above mentioned theoretical introduction states, they let the symptom itself speak. The second issue of *Punk Problemi*, published in 1982 (no. 221), slightly alters their approach towards punk, now indicating the antagonisms within the movement, especially including its "bad" faction, which was the hard-core version, then sweeping the scene with its fast, furious, and uncompromising energy. The intro to this issue was written by Mladen Dolar, the author of a psychoanalytic study of fascism, today the authority on Lacanian-formalist readings of Hitchcock, opera, voice, and popular culture. Both these short theoretical texts that give background to punk self-representation are translated here as an appendix to the broader theoretical readings.

Following Močnik and Žižek's essays comes Zoja Skušek's 'Along Came Turk …', translated from the Serbo-Croatian version published in 1981 in *Dometi*, a journal from Rijeka. This essay in no way mentions punk, and for that reason, it needs a word of justification for its inclusion in this publication. Skušek's essay is reworked from her long introduction to the anthology dedicated to Slovenian translation of Althusserian writings on aesthetics, which she edited. Apart from Althusser, the anthology also includes texts by Étienne Balibar, Pierre Macherey, and Michel Pêcheux, which were at that time obscure even to English-speaking scholars. The introduction's second part, which we also translate here, deals with nationalism, particularly with the nation formation of Slovenian identity through artistic and literary forms. Skušek's thesis is to trace the materiality of the concrete historical and political circumstances of this formation. In other words, the part we are concerned with here is the application of complex Althusserian theory on aesthetic ideology to Slovenian national formation. If I am not wrong, this will be Skušek's first text to be translated into English. Apart from editing and translating the highly influential anthology on Althusser, Skušek also wrote a book on the function of theatre as spectacle, co-founded the highly influential publishing house *Založba /*cf,* worked as a translator and an editor, and was an activist in various feminist organisations. Still, her pioneering theoretical work remains to be discovered.

Skušek applies the complex Althusserian theory of overdetermination by contradiction to the trivial subject of a newspaper topic: a deadly tired, Turkish, lumpen-proletariat 'Gastarbeiter' who causes a fatal car accident on the Yugoslavian highways while on his/her way to their native village somewhere in Anatolia. The Turk – a menace, a threat – is exposed as a core symptom of the Slovenian national canon. This anonymous immigrant worker, named Turk, is defined as a phantasm of the Other, which "concretely" lives in the aesthetic forms of national literature. More precisely the Turk, that is, the other of the Slovene, is a phantasm of evil in the national literature, which is the core matter (that which is most tangible) of nationalist linguistic ideology. Skušek's text begins with the crash, with destruction, death and annihilation, but it proposes a theoretical model which unites the scattered heterogeneous traits of national antagonisms. Turk – the Other – is the "core" uniting all Slovenes, and it does this in socialist Yugoslavia, where the equality of all nations and nationalities was guaranteed by the constitution (including also the cultural rights of Turkish nationalities living in Yugoslavia). Skušek notices this unevenness and discusses it as the archaic remnant within the contemporary reality of self-management socialism. She argues that this archaic element is mediated by class relations, and is anchored in the ideological apparatus of bourgeois civil society.

Skušek's key argument is to point at the weak link in the chain of socialist modernity when facing the remnants of ideological phantasms, such as the pre-modern image of the Turk. This image, to be clear, is not a spontaneous and folkloristic residue; it is continuously reproduced among the most elitist literary and intellectualist circles. The Turk, as melted into the assumed unconsciousness of Slovenes, is a degree zero of nation-form, characterised as transgressing both class and historical consciousness. Skušek suggests the materialist methodology that would concretize this Turk, and empty its associations from "a poetic supplement" of bourgeois literature – through this process opposing the continuous ideological unfolding of national reproduction of identity.

Both Turk and punk are symptoms of something larger, but their effects are to be measured in diametrically opposite axes. The punk of Lacanians is the symptom of dispersion, of falling apart, and of distortion; whereas the Turk of Skušek is a silent but strong current in national cohesion, waiting to be amplified in order for its contradictions to emerge. The Turk unites, the punk separates. Still, this is not the only reason for the inclusion of Skušek's text into this collection. What allows for the comparison of punk and Turk, and theoretically justifies the inclusion of Skušek's text in this collection, is the materialist and anti-institutional approach to artistic forms. It is this aspect that provided the stimulation for theoretical and political engagement with punk. The texts of all three authors published here – Močnik, Skušek, and Žižek – expand their theoretical arguments by introducing strong anti-institutional positions and avant-garde forms.

By underlining the experimental character of contemporary innovations, these texts (especially Močnik's) suggest that punk could break from the stalemate of artistic recuperation and representation. Močnik's text, the theoretical backbone of this collection, provides a direct entry point to this discourse. His analysis of "punk-form" and "punk-theory" gives the pretext to discuss punk in socialism as a new political force. If nothing else, this warrants attention. Situating punk in an explicitly political background is no new thing – the two cannot be separated. What Močnik does though, is something rather different than the usual political interpretation of punk; he interprets politics through punk. Can punk teach us something about socialist self-management, the dead ends of school reform, state contradictions, nationalism, and the autonomy of artistic forms? The same is true for Žižek, who claims that punk could be key in reading the deep traumatic kernel of self-management contradictions, and whose research on punk, as it happens, was financed by the institution researching self-management in the Socialist Republic of Slovenia. Despite their similarity in approach towards the politics of punk, and their use of the same theoretical references (Lacan, Althusser, analytical philosophy), Močnik and Žižek's conclusions regarding the usefulness of punk are quite different.

By 1984, when *Punk Pod Slovenci* was compiled, punk in Slovenia and Yugoslavia had grown into a very complicated network of subcultures. Hard-core was

then the new avant-garde of punk, and as a result
of their unprecedented organisational skills, had
formed into 'hardkor-kolektiv'. Already in 1983,
the first albums (often cassettes) of today's classic
of hard-core punk appeared: Odpadki Civilizacije,
Otroci Socijalizma, Stres Državnog Aparata, U.B.R.,
and the debut albums of experimental post-punk
and industrial bands like Via Ofanziva, O! Kult, Čao
Pičke, Abbildungen Variete, Borghesia, and Laibach.
These were all released by ŠKUC (Student Cultural
Centre), which was also a space for conceptual and
avant-garde art exhibitions, gay and lesbian activism,
and underground poetry. Parallel to this, new
alternative venues were playing all varieties of punk:
Disco Študent/Disco FV (1981–1983), Šiška Youth
Centre (1983–1984), Kersnikova 4 (K4) (1984–), and
as a result at the end of 1983, the conference called
Kaj Je Alternativa? [What is Alternative?] was organised
by ŠKUC, with support from the RK ZSMS
(Republican Conference of the Socialist Youth
League of Slovenia), wherein over a two-day event,
punks, artists, activists, and scholars had a joint
venture to discuss the pressing questions of the
underground.

    The concept of "alternativa" is difficult to
translate into English; as it is not a mere alternative,
but refers to a conglomerate of politicized and
public manifestations of civil society opposition, to
which punk gave an initial impetus. At least, this
is how Tomaž Mastnak defined and propagated it
in many of his writings, theoretically defining the
alternativa as, "an analytical concept to discuss the
oppositional (socialist) civil society, and to link it

with alternative cultural organisations (particularly punk)" ['Uzroci Represije' (Reasons of Repression), *Potkulture, no. 4*, 1988]. Močnik, on the other hand, had a more formalistic understanding of alternative, defining its eclectic style as postmodernism without baroque and retro-garde elements ("the alternative transfers the postmodernist principle upon the present itself", from the 'Postmodernism and the Alternative' lecture given in the ŠKUC Gallery in 1985). Counter to these theoretical nuances, protagonists of the movement – its activists and militants – were not happy with these definitions. For example Marjan Ogrinc-Mao, a DJ from Radio Študent, who in his account of the scene, dismissed the 'alternative' as a pacifying tendency reducing punk to "artism" and domesticating its subversion. Ogrinc was not alone in resisting the co-option of punk by civil society, which he saw as recuperation, confining punk into a enclave of the artistic avant-garde "impoverishing the potential of its social subversion" [Marjan Ogrinc, 'Ni nam do tega, da bi postali zgodovina', ('We are not Here to Become a History'), *Punk Pod Slovenci*]. He saw in hard-core collectivism an answer to this stalemate of the 'alternative'; an organised youth who took matters into their own hands. This was in 1983, the year still reverberating from the police violence against students' demonstrations in Prishtina, which split the leftist post-Marxist intellectuals on the nationalist axis; the year of the Belgrade Process against students who organised a talk by Milovan Đilas, a communist dissident; and a year when in Yugoslavia the new school reforms were discussed, which further politicised the students. While all this mass political turmoil was happening, and the youth were emerging as an oppositional political force, punk was, for a short period of time, introduced as an avant-garde of this new conjuncture.

In his text 'Reason Wins', Močnik proposes to look at the reasons for this new artistic-political alternative; to discover the form, and the theory, of this new mass movement. He introduces punk as a reversal of the stalemate of conceptual art. Punk intervenes in the field where OHO conceptualism and concrete poetry, and the 1968 spirit of sub-version reached its limits. Punk is a new principle, a new logic, argues Močnik. In this regard, Močnik's ideas were not different from the punk theory of his protagonists, from those of Ogrinc, for example, who wrote that "punk is the break". In Močnik's version of punk, these youth alternatives and underground movements not only break from the bourgeois-national-traditional concept of civil society, but also turn artistic forms, and their potential social functions, upside down. It is obvious that this observation refers to something larger than punk proper – meaning the punk of nightclubs, squats, subculture, graffiti and records – it is the ideology of the punk effect that these philosophers and theoreticians were aiming to decode. What Močnik did was to decipher the *political thought*, as contemporary Althusserians like to say, of punk. Reclaiming reason, and the logic, of punk, was an attempt to separate this new form from the liberal cynicism of anti-intellectualism, and to differentiate punk from "apolitical dissident ideology of dominant cultural elite". Giving credit to the organisational skills of punks instead of their anarcho-liberal spontaneities, was the merit of Močnik's intervention. Anyone involved in the punk scene would know that there are no better organisers, and no collectives more disciplined, than those of punk, especially its radical militant faction known as hard-core punk.

To understand the novelty of this theoretical insight, we should compare it with Žižek's interpretation of punk's cynical gesture in the face of civil society. Žižek famously wrote that "punk is the *objet petit a*", meaning, in complicated Lacanian terminology, that punk is the unattainable, unspeakable, the impossible, the asocial attitude, the excrement of the system. It is the Lacanian real, the core and the kernel of society. To this end, punk is neither interpellated into ideology, nor is it part of the language-games of social norms; it is not caught in the endless rituals of ideological reproduction. Punk is the subject beyond ideology, a "psychotic split" and "dehumanized apathy". Žižek used this last description for the industrial-punk band Laibach, whose performance in 1983, provoked an outsider journalist from the official newspaper to report it as an "infinitely nightmarish" experience. Through this metaphor, which Žižek also uses in the text we translate here, he draws further conclusions regarding the limits of the classical Marxist understanding of national ideologies. He argues for the importance of the libidinal economy in engaging with fascism, and later in 1987 famously declared the "analytical impotence before NSK [Neue Slowenische Kunst, the art collective to which Laibach band belonged] represents a defeat for Marxism" (Slavoj Žižek, 'A Letter from Afar', originally published in a weekly *Mladina*, April 1987).

In an interview with Peter Osborne, Žižek once said that "it is precisely through punk that the pluralist opposition reached the masses. It was a kind of political punk education, and we supported it" ('Lacan in Slovenia, an interview with Slavoj Žižek and Renata Salecl', *A Critical Sense: Interviews with Intellectuals*, Routledge, 1996, p. 23). During the first years of the eighties, the political background of punk was rather different than at the beginning of the nineties, when socialism in Yugoslavia no longer existed. Texts written about punk in Yugoslavia are more often about totalitarianism, understood in Yugoslavia as a latent remnant of bureaucratic Stalinism in the state which had begun to openly disavow political Stalinism by the late forties. Močnik outlines these two conflicting ideologies in Yugoslavia by separating the ideology of the ruling groups, from the ruling social ideology. The ruling ideology of Yugoslavia was "self-management ideology", whereas the ideology of power is "naively totalitarian and Stalinist". The strength of punk, according to Žižek, Močnik, Dolar, Mastnak, and many others, was in its direct intervention into this contradiction.

Stalin, in Yugoslavia, was seen as such a demanding and pressing reality that the Association of the Socialist Youth of Croatia published the translation of an eight hundred page book of Stalin,

Foundations of Leninism, in 1981. Applying Lacanian theories of four discourses, Žižek in 1982 reviewed this book claiming that Stalin, as well as Hitler, dealt with classes as "constative-performatives", and situated the class struggles within the discourse and the linguistic formations. In order to break from the classical and rigid approach we need to refresh Marx's concept of class struggle; we would need to, Žižek argues, go beyond language, and to organise the class struggle around "non-conceptualized, 'traumatic' real kernel (core)". This deep reality is the Lacanian real core, wrapped within the mist of the phantasm. Both Stalinism and Fascism, Žižek concludes, offer us the phantasm of reality instead of the real reality of an impossible and traumatic encounter with the core of our identities. Punk, according to Žižek, pierced this veiled reality and revealed the immanent "lawlessness" and tautology of the law, ultimately exposing the "infinite nightmare" of the real kernel of ideology.

At the beginning of the eighties, in Slovenia, the real problem of punk was not Stalinism, but Fascism. In October 1981 the Ljubljana weekly *Nedeljni Tjednik* published a text called 'Who draws Swastikas?', accusing punks as the culprit for this action, and stigmatizing punks as apolitical nihilists, anarcho-liberals, and in worst cases mis-guided exponents of the Western neo-nazi youth. Punk was soon associated with fascism in almost all Yugoslav press; to oppose this mass hysteria, student unions, intellectuals, theoreticians, socio-logists, journalists, and in the end the Minister of Culture, organised public discussions on the relationship between punk and fascism. This is the so-called 'Nazi-Punk Affair' in Yugoslavia. *Punk Pod Slovenci*, reproduced almost all documents related to this mass outcry. Following this scandal, Igor Vidmar, promoter and organiser of punk in Slovenia, was interrogated by the police as he was spotted wearing a swastika badge next to a sickle and hammer, and a badge saying "Crazy Government". Preceding this was the so-called 'Laibach Affair', referring to the appearance of Laibach in 1983 in Zagreb Music Biennial, and the subsequent TV interview where the band wore military-style uniforms and Malevich influenced symmetric insignias, reminiscent of totalitarian Nazi aesthetics. Laibach had a complicated theory of over-identification, which Močnik also discusses in his article on punk, underlining the political strategy of their aesthetics based on emptying out the remnants of totalitarian ideologies that they argued were still haunting socialist Yugoslavia.

Žižek saw this extremity in a larger frame; interpreting the machine-like punk gesture as a commentary on ideological subjectivation. Moreover, as Žižek argued in another text, Laibach's dehumanized apathy and surrender to the ideological ritual of self-management produces a much more powerful estrangement than an ironic approach towards the system. Unfortunately, instead of the intended effect of estrangement, the audience, including hard-core punks, often experienced Laibach's performative rituals of ideological exorcism as an ambiguity towards politics, disregarding their subversive gesture (which was a gesture similar to other industrial-punk bands like Throbbing Gristle, toying with fascism), as a confused extremism, an 'artism'. In Žižek's narrative, the expected result of this subversion, the "infinitely nightmarish" experience of punk performance, is presented as something like the abject energy of society splitting the self-managing cynical subject, which as a result was manifesting the scars – the trauma – of the socialist identity. The 'punk model' of Žižek is based on repetition and mimicry of the forms of ruling and dominant ideology, and as such, the cynicism of punk, and its subversive effect, is no more subversive and cynical than the "provocation employed by the authorities". The implication of this conclusion is, as Žižek himself notes in the conclusion to the text we publish here, that the Authorities themselves are the real Great Punks. Ultimately, punk is the artistic model of inauthenticity – the unnatural, unrelaxed, and tense social attitude. Žižek is right in seeing this attitude, as opposed to the hippy pose of spontaneity, and interpreting the machinic-form of punk as a more advanced model of ideological struggle. But it is completely misguided to see punks as a symptom of a "psychotic split" of madness and of inherently compulsive paranoia.

On the other hand, the distinctiveness of punks, as Močnik has argued, indicates the "truly creative and self-organisational capacities of the oppressed youth masses".This observation alone deserves a full theoretical treatise, which Močnik delivers by introducing reason, logic, and theory as devices to oppose the anti-intellectualist cynicism of the cultural bureaucracy. What is then the punk theory? The sociological approach is too limited to encounter the complexities of this form; one needs a more nuanced version of the ideological operations that would orient within the dialectics between the ruling ideology and the ideology of rulers. Močnik argues for an anti-Stalinist theory that would be non-universal, in other words, a theory of non-identity and anti-institutional thought. This was a domain traditionally reserved for avant-garde and contemporary art, which by then, had relapsed into the bureaucratic cultural elitism of "artistic autonomy". It is only the masses of dispossessed youth who are able to melt the ice of this stalemate and introduce the new forms. With their organisational skills and detachment from the existing language of the cultural elite, the punks are doubtless the avant-garde of this tendency. Punk is the avant-garde mass culture; the counter-force against the consumerism of liberal ideologies and the mortified bureaucracy of art institutions. To engage with this novelty, or write about these practices, as Močnik wittily observes, requires practising some sort of "punk theory", which in reality means the abandonment of self-satisfied intellectualist distance and involvement with a "materialist theory of the Maoist lunacy". This is the extremity to which we are subscribing: punk as a cultural revolution of non-institutional youth anger! Močnik should be credited for this definition of punk as a cultural force, more modern than modernity, and more advanced than the avant-garde.

In theory, this is true, but in reality, and in politics, punk does not necessarily subscribe to this radical anti-institutional realm. In conclusion, Močnik observes that Pankrti, the first punk band in Yugoslavia, threatens to slip into "passive harmonious artistry", while Laibach succumbs into "unhinged activism". As Tomaž Mastnak was later reminiscing, the first use of civil society as a political and theoretical category in Slovenia, appeared in the already mentioned 'What is Alternative?' symposium, organized by a collaboration of post-Marxist philosophers and punks. In the eighties, civil society was still an amorphous category, soon to evolve into a large umbrella of the socialist civil society including all kinds of advocates of identity politics, nationalists, anti-communists, quasi-religious groups, punks, and dissidents of all colours and shades. By the mid-eighties, as Mastnak himself has argued, the struggle between civil society and the state had transformed into the struggle between non-democratic and democratic civil society. This, in practice, meant that socialism and communism did not have any political and theoretical mandate in discussing the oppositional alternative forms of punk. As Gregor Tomc, the first punk sociologist and advocate of liberalism in Slovenia argued, the "contribution of punks to the downfall of the socialist revolution" was not a negligible issue. During this political downfall and the moment of counter-revolution, Žižek, cynically mimicking Lenin, wrote in his already mentioned 'Letter from Afar', that Marxism cannot explain "phantasmatic myths and constructs on which our national identification is based". Neither Marxism nor Semiotics can, within their analytical tools, contain the "sprouts of pleasure", which Laibach is successfully mobilizing. Žižek, in that text from the late eighties, preferred "infinite nightmarish" expressions to the "appeals to reason", and introduced the psycho-political concepts yet unprecedented neither in socialist Yugoslavia nor anywhere in the world.

Mastnak, then leading theoretician of socialist civil society, opposed Žižek's insistence on the "irrational", underlining the fact that he is under-valuing the political (institutional) gains of civil society's contribution to struggle against totalitarianism, and is silencing the democratic potential of civil society movements in Slovenia. In addition to this, as someone knowledgeable of the scene, Mastnak emphasized the fact that the punk and alternative scene in Slovenia was not only about Laibach and NSK; that these movements and initiatives, and, as he wrote, "institutions", live autonomously, "not only in relation to politics and the state but also in relation to each other" (Mastnak, 'On the Soul of Social Movements: A Few Remarks from Up Close on Žižek's Letter from Afar', originally published in *Mladina*, April 1987). These murky debates were the beginnings of the long march towards taking over the state institutions, a struggle which continues in Slovenia – even in 2021 – among the different actors of the civil society protagonists from the eighties!

As already mentioned, the analysis of Zoja Skušek has introduced "the poetic supplement" as a concept to delineate the "productive" aspect of national ideology. Specifically referring to the production, and the reproduction, of the national subjects through artistic ideology, Skušek's idea was to expose the fact that the nation, in order to reproduce itself, needs something else to add, some supplement, which in this case was carried through the excessive force of the image of Turk, corresponding to the image of the other. In punk, this operation is rather upside down. The punk intervention in the eighties has created a cut in the ideological and political environment of socialist Yugoslavia, especially, as it is discussed here, in the Socialist Republic of Slovenia. We need another kind of poetic supplement that could provide us with an entry into the punk's singularity. Punk, especially its hard-core version, defended a complete detachment from normative bourgeois values of society; they were negating, denying, destroying, and absolutely refusing the existing social norms. With their dehumanized, catatonic, ritualistic, mechanistic, violent, non-communicating, underground, strong, and hard-core forms they were for absolute detachment; a sort of autopoietic subjective form relying solely on its own forces. Punk needed no representation, no mediation. Everything was necessary and arbitrary at the same time; it emerged from nowhere and was not leading anywhere. It is similar to Kazimir Malevich's suprematist figures, "standing without windows and doors ... not seeking any goods or expedient things no business benefit from ideas, no 'promised' lands" (Malevich, 'Suprematism

[1927]', *The Artist, Infinity, Suprematism: Unpublished Writings*, Borgen, Copenhagen, 1978). In the twenties, pressed from the political background of communism, but still insisting on the non-representable and non-utilitarian aspect of the 'black square', Malevich introduced a new concept, *the additional element*, which he defined as an "element exercising a strong influence on the attitude of the artist toward the life roundabout him/her (even in respect to economics and politics)" [Malevich, *The Non-Objective World*, p. 60].

The nihilistic attitude of punk in Slovenia was also pressed by the strong influence from economics and politics, and as well from the ideology, to reconsider its course in the turbulent period during the fall of socialism. This is the case in all other republics in Yugoslavia (particularly in Croatia and Serbia), but as well as in other socialist countries like Poland, Czechoslovakia, Hungary, and the Soviet Union. What was specific with punk in Slovenia was, first of all, the originality of its form and music, whose songs are still today covered by hard-core punk bands throughout the world, and second, the existence of theoreticians who engaged with this new unprecedented form. The philosophers' contribution to this new conjuncture was to find the right conceptual terms to engage with the additional element; the element which emerged after the crash of punk with the society. The novel forms they were detecting in punk were unlike the forms and devices of the canonic and contemporary artistic productions. It was new and outside. This capacity of punk gave a new route to the theory; as it can be read in the following essays. Some of the actual concepts of Žižek, now arguably in more domesticated versions, were first tested in the realm of punk. We might not agree with Žižek's conclusion that punk is the "*objet petit a*" of the socialist psycho-politics negating the additional element of social imperative; but, regardless of the absurdity of this speculation, still, it is historical evidence highlighting the force of punk.

Močnik, in his theoretical treatise of punk, gave a completely different entry into the additional element of punk transformation; it was the possibility of the new cultural revolution emancipated both from the traditional remnants of the bureaucratic culture, the elitist dead-end of artistic autonomy, the passivity of non-antagonistic contradiction of civil society, and the unhinged activism of anarchist subversion. Punk's distinction indicated, as Močnik writes, the "truly creative and self-organisational capacities of the oppressed youth masses". Althusserian Maoist lunacy, with its radical materialist conceptions, which continues to be a defining parameter of contemporary philosophy, is closest to this "punk theory", of which Močnik is speculating about. Without organisation, discipline, and the collective spirit, which are the additional elements of punk, this hard-core gesture would not correspond to the realities of our times.

The Narrative Bibliography of Punk in the Socialist Republic of Slovenia in the Eighties

The single most important source for studying punk in Slovenia in the eighties is *Punk Pod Slovenci* [Punk Under Slovenians], edited by Nela Malečkar and Tomaž Mastnak. The book was published in 1985 by ZSMS (Socialist Youth League of Slovenia), in a run of 3000 copies, in their KRT series, wherein each of its publications bore a quotation from Brecht, "The book is a weapon, therefore take it in your hands". *Punk Pod Slovenci* is a dense, small-format book of 542 pages. It is divided into three parts: analyses, documents, and testimonies. Rastko Močnik's article we translate here is taken from the 'analyses' section, and it also includes texts by Gregor Tomc, a sociological study of the formation of punk in Slovenia, and a detailed presentation of the then ongoing ideological struggles; Andreja Potokar's social anthropology of punks in Ljubljana based on interviews, predictable in its conclusions, the text has some memorable quotes from punks, such as one saying that "In Ljubljana punk was until 1981, after that it's only alternative". There is an obscure text by Peter Mlakar, 'Svetonazorski Princip Punka', which could be translated as Weltanschauungsprinzip of punk. Influenced by German philosophy, Mlakar was the founder of the Department of Pure and Applied Philosophy at the Neue Slowenische Kunst collective and he was a member of Laibach, his philosophy is based on eclectic postmodern Nietzscheanism. Marjan Ogrinc's subjective contribution is one of the most interesting statements regarding punk self-

historicisation. The principal thesis of his essay 'We Don't Want to Become History', is to argue for punk as a break, and to defend hard-core as the ultimate form of punk. 'Mao', as he was known, is still a cult punk figure in Slovenia, he acted himself in Želimir Žilnik's *Stara Mašina* in 1989. The 'documents' part of the book is the most interesting, and the most exhaustive section. It reproduces almost all important documents (statements, newspaper clips, transcripts of discussions, interviews, inquiries) related to punk in Slovenia from 1977 to 1984, focusing especially on the first years of the eighties. The sources are from the official press and as well from fanzines. There are early statements of *Rock Front*, mostly written and spoken by Igor Vidmar, an early protagonist of punk in Yugoslavia, and the discussions related to Laibach's eponymous appearance in Trbovlje. From 1981 onwards there are more frequent commentaries of the youth socialist association (ZSMS) which were publishers of *Punk Pod Slovenci*; these are the most valuable and concrete documents on the ideology of punk. On reading these ideological discussions one can have a clearer picture of the socialist institutions' reaction towards punk: it was much more open and engaging than the official anti-communist narratives of today are ready to accept. Especially interesting are contributions by Srečo Kirn, then the president of the commission for ideological-political work under RK ZSMS. There are plenty of reprints from the press materials accusing punks of being Neo-nazis, which was initiated by

The Narrative Bibliography of Punk in the Socialist Republic of Slovenia in the Eighties

Nedeljski Dnevnik's article 'Who is Drawing Swastikas?', published on 22 November 1981. Almost all theoreticians, punk protagonists, politicians, and organizers' have commented on this article. All these documents, including the all-Yugoslavian press, are reproduced in *Punk Pod Slovenci*. This follows with discussions mostly related to the question "what is punk?", and its political consequences. The majority of documents from 1983 onwards are related to the Laibach Affair, the band's appearance in Zagreb Music Biennial and in the following TV interview. 1983 was also a year of 'alternative', including more frequent theoretical and intellectual commentaries on punk. It is also a year when hard-core emerged as a stronger force in the punk scene. The 'testimonies' – the last and the shortest sections of the book, reproduce interviews with punks originally published in various newspapers and magazines.

The second important source for punk studies are the three issues of *Punk Problemi*, dedicated to punk. Slavoj Žižek, Rastko Močnik, Mladen Dolar, Rado Riha and other Lacanians and Althusserians were its editors. The first *Punk Problemi* was published in 1981 (no. 205-206) and has a short intro by Žižek about "punk-as-symptom", as well as longer texts by Gregor Tomc, Peter Mlakar, translations of texts on Sex Pistols, photo-novellas on punk lives, the underground comics, and lyrics of Yugoslav punk bands. The second issue of *Punk Problemi* was published in 1982 (no. 221) and is edited by Mladen Dolar, who wrote a short

introduction giving a new theoretical framework for punk. The graphics (comics, posters, collages) are more experimental, the reproduction of Yugoslav punk bands' lyrics are more fanzine-like, the whole issue is influenced by the S/M and gey aesthetics, dominating with Laibach-Kunst style. Igor Vidmar, Gregor Tomc, and Peter Mlakar also have texts within the issue. Tomc's text 'Apocalyptic Heaven', defends punk as an apolitical and non-ideological youth movement with the tendency towards anarchism, which he presents as against discipline, order, authority, flag, etc. The third issue of *Punk Problemi* was published in 1983 (no. 236), it is a split issue including a performative special section of Radio Študent on the 'military state'. The third issue is the most Laibach oriented, it was edited by two NSK members, Peter Mlakar and Dušan Mandić. Includes also lyrics of Borghesia, O! Kult, Esad Babačić-Car, and other post-punk bards and musicians.

Problemi published about punk in other regular issues as well, for example one by Žižek in 1984, from where we translated 'A Few Thoughts About the Issue of the Ideological Presuppositions of Punk' (No. 1-3, 1984). In 1985, the whole issue of *Problemi* was dedicated to Neue Slowenische Kunst (No. 254). Other theoretical and critical journals like *Časopis za Kritiko Znanosti*, *Nova Revija*, have also published writings engaging with punk. Most notably, *Nova Revija*, issue 13/14, 1983, published Laibach's manifesto, and the literary critique Taras Kermanuer's long study of Laibach-Kunst, 'X + (-) = ?'.

The Narrative Bibliography of Punk in the Socialist Republic of Slovenia in the Eighties

Another source of content about punk in Slovenia is ŠKUC releases. From June 1981 to May 1984, ŠKUC released 27 zines, cassettes, and books. Mostly edited by Marina Gržinić, these were often printed in 50 or 100 copies. The third serial publication is dedicated to the 'Relationship of the Ruling Ideology to Subcultures', edited by Gržinić and Aina Šmid, and is a disclaimer against the state provocations aligning punk politics with fascism and neo-nazism. Most of ŠKUC zines have reproduced punk lyrics (Esad Babačić-Car, Ivo Frančić), artistic collages, photos from gigs, which also included cassettes. Between 1983-85, ŠKUC-Forum published four issues of A4 size fanzine *VIKS*, mostly edited by Gržinić in collaboration with Dušan Mandić. The first issue on 'Violence and Representation' was published in November 1983 includes text by Vito Oražem, 'On Eros of Photocopying', Aina Šmid's 'Fashion in the Function of Mass Culture', Zamira Alajbegović's 'Youth Subculture – Disko FV – No Future – No Escape', about underground multimedia activities at Disko FV, a collage on Laibach-Kunst, Gržinić's interview with Dick Hebdige – whose *Subculture: Meaning of Style* appeared in Serbo-Croatian translation in Yugoslavia in 1980. The second issue of *VIKS* was 'Homo-sexuality and Culture', published in April 1984; the third issue 'On Postmodernism and Retroprinciple', published in February 1985; the fourth, final, issue was published in December 1985 with the title 'People Pricking Like Thorns'. The third issue of *VIKS* carried an interview with Tomaž Mastnak, discussing the political and ideological consequences of demonizing punks in Slovenia. The future apologist of the (socialist) civil society claims that the hard-core punk's "non-democratic, and non-tolerant practices" should be understood differently from its normative (bourgeois) meaning. Mastnak argues that punk is the first mass movement that anticipated the novelty of the actual conjuncture – the "spirit of the time" – before anyone else did.

Some of the most important writings on punk by Slovenian theoreticians, activists, and art historians are collected in the recent anthology dedicated to the activities of Neue Slowenische Kunst, *NSK: From Kapital to Capital*, edited by Zdenka Badovinac, Eda Čufer, and Anthony Gardner, published by the MIT Press in 2015. It includes texts by Žižek, 'Ideology, Cynicism, Punk', (originally published in *Filozofija Skozi Psihoanalizo [Philosophy through Psychoanalysis]*, 1984), Močnik, 'Postmodernism and the Alternative' (originally given as a talk at ŠKUC Gallery in 1985), Mastnak 'On the Soul of Social Movement', Dolar 'Psychoanalysis in Power: On Fascism, Marxism and the Poster Scandal' (both published in 1987 in the weekly *Mladina*). Unfortunately, most of the literature about punk in Slovenia is dominated by Laibach. Further materials can be found in other NSK related publications. Žižek's 'A Letter from Afar' (1987), 'Why are Laibach and NSK not Fascists?' (1993), and 'The Enlightenment in Laibach' (1994) are included in *Irwin Retroprincip,*

The Narrative Bibliography of Punk in the Socialist Republic of Slovenia in the Eighties

edited by Inke Arns (Revolver – Archive fur Aktuelle Kunst, Frankfurt am Main, 2003). The same *Irwin Retroprincip* includes also Mladen Dolar's short commentary titled, 'On the Punk Movement and the Rituals of Ideology' (2003). Močnik's gloomy structuralist lecture given in 1992 in Moscow on the political dead-ends of the Slovenian alternative, 'How We Were Fighting for the Victory of Reason and What Happened When We Made It', was published in another NSK catalogue (*NSK Embassy Moscow*, 1992). There is the MIT Press book, fully dedicated on this subject, written by Alexei Monroe, *Interrogation Machine: Laibach and NSK* (The MIT, 2005, part of Short Circuit series edited by Žižek), a theoretical speculation on totalitarian culture mostly based on the readings of English language art-related documents.

There are also publications dealing more generously with punk groupations other than Laibach. Alenka Barber-Kersovan's *Vom "Punk-Frühling" zum "Slowenischen Fruhling"* [From "Punk Spring" to "Slovenian Spring"], published in Hamburg in 2005 (Krämer Press). It is a 577 page book with a very rich overview of the punk movement in Slovenia in the eighties, extending its historical spectrum all the way to the fall of socialism. The book argues for the political aspect of punk by detailing its trajectory, via civil society, into independent Slovenia. Barber-Kersovan reviewed *Punk Pod Slovenci* for scholarly journal *Popular Music* (Volume 6, issue 3, October 1987), and that is the only information

available on this book in the English language. Marina Gržinić also wrote retrospectively about punk, where she links punk to the contemporary art world, postmodernism and civil society, and interprets the punk ideology through Žižek's lenses of Lacanian phantasms on self-management cynicism. In her 'Punk: strategy, politics and amnesia' text written in 2005, Gržinić memorably writes that "before punk, Ljubljana was a village; with the emergence of punk it became a city", a statement that is difficult not to agree with (Published in *Estetika Kibersvijeta i Učinci Derealizacije* [Aesthetics of Cyberspace and the Effects of Derealisation], Multimedijalni Institut, Zagreb, 2005) . The only scholarly article in English, so far, dedicated to the theoretical writings on punk in Slovenia is by Helena Matoh, '"Punk is a Symptom": Intersection of Philosophy and Alternative Culture in the 80's Slovenia', published in *Synthesis Philosophica, No. 54*, in 2012. It is, again, a Žižek centred analysis misreading the Lacanian influence, claiming that punk strategy was an "ideological falsity" based on "irony and sarcasm that targeted the hypocrisy of the ruling ritual".

Perhaps one of the most interesting retrospective publications on punk and alternative scene in Slovenia is a catalogue of the exhibition *FV : alternativa osemdesetih / alternative scene of the eighties*, realized and published by mglc: Mednarodni grafični likovni center (International Centre of Graphic Arts) in Ljubljana in 2008. The exhibition is mostly based on Neven Korda's private archives,

The Narrative Bibliography of Punk in the Socialist Republic of Slovenia in the Eighties

who also wrote an exhaustive and brilliant historical analysis of the formation of punk alternative in Ljubljana in the eighties. Being a member of Borghesia, a multimedia industrial punk band, Korda gave a first-hand account of the scene, including the complicated relationship with the socialist institutions, and the exciting objective presentation of the emergence of the hard-core punk collective. Definitely, the most reliable source yet printed on this subject.

Literature about punk in Slovenia is often linked with discussions on the independence of Slovenia. There are two articles on punk in the scholarly book *Independent Slovenia: Origins, Movements, Prospects* (St. Martin Press, London, 1994, edited by Jill Benderly). Tomaž Mastnak's 'From Social Movements to National Sovereignty', argues for the revisionist thesis that the destruction of "the balance of public discourse in Yugoslavia" started with Serbian nationalist "anti-punk campaign", whereas Gregor Tomc's explicitly anti-communist article 'The Politics of Punk' defends punk-rock subversion of Pankrti against "politics" of Laibach. The subchapter in Tomc's article is titled 'The Contribution of Punk to the Downfall of the Socialist Revolution'. Tomc in fact took an active part in accelerating this downfall by joining the group of reactionary intellectuals who co-authored 'Prispevki za slovenski nacionalni program (Contributions to the Slovene National Program)' in *Nova Revija, No. 57* in 1987, the Slovenian dissidents' programme for national renewal. There are two theoretical texts discussing this shift from socialism to nationalism via the civil society, within the larger ideological frame of post-Marxism. Ozren Pupovac, 'Springtime for Hegemony: Laclau and Mouffe with Janez Janša' (*Prelom, No. 8*, 2006), showing the theoretical and political myopia of 'radical and plural democracy' thesis; Slobodan Karamanić, 'Totaliteta, Partijnost, Slovenci' ('Totality, Partisanship, Slovenians', *Borec, No. 672-675*, 2010), systematically exposing the contribution of Lacanian post-Marxism in Slovenia to the downfall of socialism.

REASON WINS[1]
Rastko Močnik

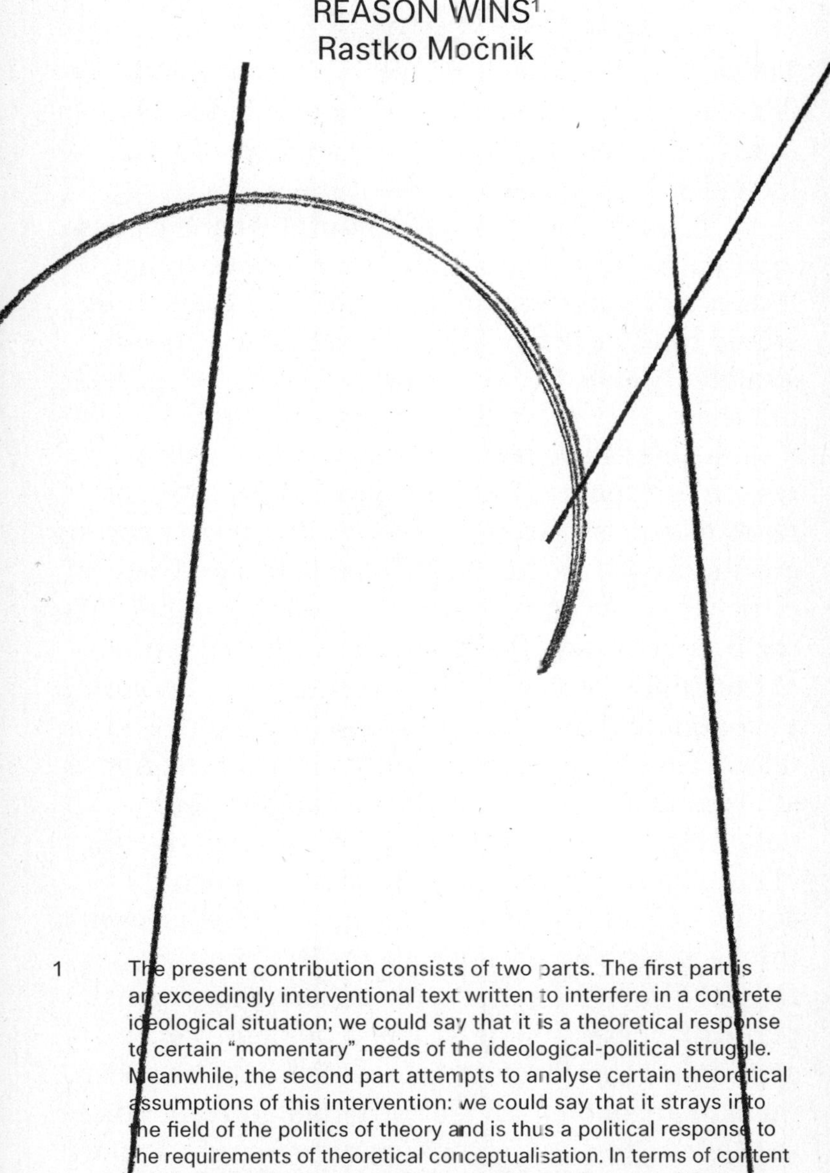

1   The present contribution consists of two parts. The first part is an exceedingly interventional text written to interfere in a concrete ideological situation; we could say that it is a theoretical response to certain "momentary" needs of the ideological-political struggle. Meanwhile, the second part attempts to analyse certain theoretical assumptions of this intervention: we could say that it strays into the field of the politics of theory and is thus a political response to the requirements of theoretical conceptualisation. In terms of content and form, the title motto actually only fits the first part of the text, yet we have nevertheless decided to use it as the title of the text in its entirety – in order not to encourage the idealistic impression that theory is anything but a momentary political intervention, as if theory floated in some sort of eternal blessed waters; as well as because we believe that the title motto is still valid.

The intention of the titular phrase "reason wins" is not to ply us with naïve enlightenment illusions, nor is it supposed to lull us into any sort of intellectualised arrogance.

"Reason wins" is an ascertainment and assessment of the actual situation. It is also a warning: it does not make any sense to pretend to be more stupid than we in fact are. If we do not use reason, somebody else will: reason will win in both cases, but the victory will not necessarily be ours.

Insofar as we still live in an enlightened society, reason is a general ideology of the times. And as far as reason is a general ideology, it is also a neutral ground for ideological conflicts. Based on the criticism of the enlightened position that underlines the bourgeois and the historically limited nature of the Enlightenment, it is nevertheless not possible to conclude that in case of ideological conflicts, reason should be given up already in advance. Above all, reason as a means of class struggle should definitely not be denounced in times when the rule of bureaucracy constantly threatens to push the entirety of society towards the pre-bourgeois level. Intellectuals have always been prone to sentimentally mythologising the spontaneous movements of the dispossessed masses; and no matter how appropriate this ideological tactic is for the establishment of an ideological platform that corresponds to the low level of the mass consciousness, it can become a dangerous trick if the intellectuals fall for it themselves. Namely, the mythologisation of spontaneity then becomes a reason for the intellectuals to renounce the only thing that they can contribute to the struggle for progress and simply fail in the struggle of the very masses that they mythologise.

This is something that we should constantly keep in mind when analysing the contemporary movements of the dispossessed youth masses. These masses have not been dispossessed merely in a directly "economical" way, but also ideologically – they have been deprived of "culture" or "sophistication" as the capacity to establish their own ideological (class-related) platform based on the progressive historical legacy. It is almost superfluous to once again argue in favour of this claim by describing the most recent move in the class struggle of the bureaucracy: school reform, the main goals of which include the severance of the youth from the historic acquisition of previous formations, and the youth's deprivation from ideological weapons that are developed in the social sciences and humanities, headed by philosophy.

In this situation, **punk** in its distinctive form that has developed in Slovenia indicates the truly creative and self-organisational capacities of the oppressed youth masses. However, we need to be realistic in this admission: punk and the entire "alternative" that surrounds it are nevertheless a movement of the culturally dispossessed masses that face the callous ruling ideology in its most material form in school or at work. The only ideology that these masses are familiar with is the one that they legitimately hate: the ruling ideology.

The youth masses are thus up against a wall. Seemingly, they do not have any possibility to assert themselves ideologically as a socio-historical subject: they have been denied the tools for the creation of their own societal bonds.

In such a situation, the punk twist is, naturally, downright ingenious, as the youth can "cobble together" their ideology from the miserly elements that they have at their disposal and which are hostile to them. It involves the utterly serious adoption of the very ruling ideology that oppresses the youth and that is simultaneously being cynically manipulated by the rulers themselves. This twist subverts the cynicism of contemporary bureaucratic rule.

However, no matter how clever, it should nevertheless not be mystified, as it is, in a sense, **the only possibility**. The danger in the position of today's alternative is precisely in the fact that there are no alternatives.

What are the socio-historical class presuppositions of this clash between the cynicism of the rulers and the sternness of the alternative as an "unreserved" identification with the rituals of the ruling ideology?

It would be naïve and truly narrow-mindedly enlightened to suppose that the cynical strategy of contemporary bureaucracy is some sort of a completely conscious manipulation – that bureaucracy first asks itself "how to rule" and then answers: "Ah! With cynicism, because that's the best way to screw people over." It has often been underlined that the cynicism of bureaucracy is based on the discursive strategy that is, in a way, spontaneous. However, what are the grounds for the spontaneity of this ideological operation?

This cynical operation stems from the fact that **the ideology of the ruling groups does NOT equal the ruling social ideology**.

The ideology of the bureaucratic groups that have lately been increasingly successful at assuming power is still naively totalitarian and Stalinist. Meanwhile, the ruling ideology as it is embodied in the legal-political superstructure and at least in some of the state's ideological apparatuses is the self-management ideology.

The cynical distance – the fact that the bureaucracy "does not believe" in self-management – is guaranteed by the objective position of the bureaucracy as well by its subjective self-perception. The condition for the success of this strategy is, naturally, that the bureaucracy manages to instil its **disbelief** in the existing legal-political system in the masses it rules; that it manages to induce political **apathy** in the masses. Of course, this is largely ensured by the very material **institutional** existence of the self-management ideology, insofar as it causes the internal self-blockade of democratic processes (complicated and long-winded procedures; the constant normative alteration of the procedures; the prior fragmentation of the democratic base and the incapacity for the establishment of horizontal connections; the general conservative nature of the system that does not elect project leaders but rather people as representatives of the existing system; etc.).

Whereas the cynical discursive strategy of power "spontaneously" and automatically arises from the incongruity between the ideology of the rulers and the ruling ideology, the alternative "pose" of identifying with the ideological rituals and symbols that **are impossible** to "spontaneously" identify with calls for creative effort. This effort nevertheless requires a certain minimal ideological foundation that also allows for a minimal reflection on these actions. Therefore, the contradiction between the ideology of the rulers and the ruling ideology that constitutes the strategy of power corresponds to, on the side of the alternative, the contradiction between both faces of the alternative that Slavoj Žižek has underlined (in the article '*Samoupravljanje, cinizem in punk*', Tribuna No. 2, 1984): the contradiction between the naïve anarcho-libertarian moment that functions like "resistance" as well as a certain "authentic" stance – and the moment of identifying with what cannot be identified with, i.e. with the totalitarian rituals and symbols. This second moment can no longer be mystified as the ideology of authenticity or genuineness: it does not function as resistance against the system, but rather as a refusal of the system, an asocial truth of socialisation.

The alternative paradox lies in the fact that both of these moments are as contradictory as they are a precondition for each other. Without the identification pose, the anarcho-libertarian dimension would slip back into the *authentic* and *spontaneous* ideologies of the 1960s; while without the anarcho-libertarian moment, totalitarian identification would not exist at all.

There is more to this paradox: although the true subversive moment lies in the "impossible" identification, the progressive moment can be found in the anarcho-libertarian position, which may be anachronistic in itself; yet it is not strange that it contains a progressive element, as for the today's alternative, anarcho-libertarianism is the only thing that remains of the past – namely, of the progressive historical tradition.

The internal tension in the ideological platform of today's alternative can therefore be preserved only if we conceive of both these moments together: the naïve-libertarian and the reflective-totalitarian moment.

The subversiveness of this ideology can only be preserved if we preserve its internal segmentation and inherent contradiction without attempting to play one element of the contradiction against the other. If we consider the issue in this manner, we soon glimpse the internal logic of the empirical apparitions on the alternative scene:

1. Two identifications are possible on the side of mimicking the rituals of the **ideology of the rulers**:

a) a Nazi-fascist totalitarian identification that corresponds to the corporatist moment in the ideology of the rulers;

b) a Stalinist identification that corresponds to the orthodox bureaucratic version.

2. On the side of mimicking the rituals of the **ruling ideology**, two versions are mostly possible:

a) the social-democratic version that builds on the enlightened humanist moment of the ruling ideology;

b) the pornographic-sexist version that corresponds to the objective economistic-consumer moment of the ruling ideology and thus also to the individual psychological response to this interpellation.

3. Based on the identification with the individual **addressee**, we could establish a third section, consisting of two items: the subject of interpellation of the ruling ideology and the subject of interpellation of the ideology of the rulers:

a) the subject of interpellation of the spontaneous sensualistic market economy ideology is represented by the porno-sexist version, which actually reveals the dark side of the ideology from the 1960s;

b) while the identification with the subject of interpellation of both totalitarian ideologies is represented by the sadomasochistic version.

Even though we have arrived at this scheme completely deductively, it is possible to find concrete examples for each of these items. However, we will refrain from that, as categorisation and labelling are not our intent here. The point is elsewhere: namely, in the fact that the irreducible and contradictory internal segmentation of what is too generally referred to as the alternative scene is in fact a **practical analysis** of the structure of the dominant culture. This is an analysis at the level of sensually explicit artistic practices – and therefore it can also be **practically** functional insofar as the non-theoretical sensually explicit level is precisely the level on which the dominant culture functions socially.

HOWEVER: all of these positions at the level of **declarative contents** would be impossible without a minimal theorisation at the **declarative**

position level. This minimal theorisation, which is simultaneously a minimal historical reflection, is made possible precisely by the anarcho-libertarian moment, which is, at the declarative level, the common "naive ideological" precondition for these positions. It is precisely this minimal theorisation that allows for the creative artistic effort of the alternative pose. Naturally, from the theoretical standpoint, this theorisation is truly as minimal as possible. However, this theoretical minimalism is virtually necessary and enforced:

1. Pragmatic necessity: insofar as all these alternative positions contain some social activism, it is pragmatically necessary that they operate "artistically", i.e. non-theoretically. This is the only way in which they can have a socially subversive effect, as genuine theoretical activity is so far above the level of the dominant culture that it simply cannot touch it: as it is isolated already in advance.

2. Socio-historical necessity: insofar as all these alternative positions contain a moment of social activism, their purpose is to take hold of the masses. Meanwhile, the masses cannot be taken hold of if we do not speak their language: i.e. the language of the culturally dispossessed, which is necessarily theoretically minimalistic.

We could also add a third reason onto these two: that the proponents of alternative practices cannot communicate in any other way as they themselves are part of the culturally dispossessed masses. This is a historically enforced moment in the primitivism of the alternative. The relationship between the alternative and the theory is therefore contradictory, at least if we look at it from the viewpoint of the alternative: the alternative **cannot exist** without theory, but it is **unable** to theorise on its own.

Therefore the theory needs to be introduced to the masses – and to the alternative – **from outside**. Nowadays, theory is, as it happens, the only alternative insofar as it is the only impossible alternative.

It suffices to define the theoretical moment in a completely minimal enlightened manner: as "reason". Nowadays, the ideological mechanisms of domination influence "reason". The leftist deviation would have been to therefore succumb to anti-intellectualism: anti-intellectualism is the precise strategy of power and belongs to the same category as the cultural dispossession of the masses and the instilment of political apathy in the masses. Hence, it is not unusual that those who carry out the functions of the ruling elites in the field of intellectual activities – the educational technicians of domination and the publishing regulators of ideological mechanisms – are among the loudest and most rabid practitioners of anti-intellectualism.

The anti-intellectualism of the cultural bureaucracy is one of the most important operations in its specific strategy of cynicism, which supplements the cynicism of the political bureaucracy. As we know, it is the very apolitical dissident ideology that dominates the cultural elite: they "do not believe" in self-management and "do not engage" in politics – and thus supplement the political strategy of the political bureaucracy in the specific cultural, i.e. ideological, field.

The question is whether this "dissident" position of the cultural bureaucracy is not much more dangerous than the position of that small intellectual group whose task is to fill the gap between the ideology of the rulers and the ruling ideology – and whose portrait was outlined so efficiently by Tomaž Mastnak in the *Mladina* weekly.[2] While the activities of this legitimising "intelligentsia" still encompass the naive ideological mystification of the traditional sort, the actions of the dissident cultural bureaucracy already constitute a modern strategy of the cynicism of the rulers. Therefore it is not strange that it is this precise ideology that pervades the dominant positions in today's (Slovenian) culture.

In the sense of a simple power strategy, Hitler, who represented naive anti-intellectualism, said the following: "Some of you blame me for banning the Communist Party; but I also forbade all other parties."

The Stalinist strategy does the same thing, but at a higher level – at the level of cynicism, which already requires an intellectual mind: "Bourgeois democracy is an estranged form of asserting people's freedom; if we abolish bourgeois democracy, we will thus eliminate a form of people's estrangement. The abolishment of bourgeois democracy is not an attack against freedom – quite the opposite, it is what **makes** true freedom **possible**."

2   Referring to Tomaž Mastnak's text '*Alternativa je kurba ali: Freiheit ist immer Freiheit der Andersdenkenden*', published in weekly *Mladina, No. 9*, 1984, which was a response to the collectively written text 'Hard core' published in the same issue of *Mladina*. [Ed. note]

This ideological strategy that first descends from the general abstract to the concrete and then once again soars to the general concrete and specific class rule over the general society cannot be dealt with if we renounce the intellectual mind.

In a television show, Jože Vogrinc (a sociologist and editor of *Tribuna* student weekly) tried to convince the other members of the discussion that rock was folk music and that it should, as such, not be comprehended under the auspices of music as a sort of an abstract generality – that, quite the opposite, its long existence should give rise to well-based doubts whether the *Musica sub specie* of some sort of a unified *artis liberalis* existed at all. The fact that the members of the television debate did not show much understanding for such words may be banal and predictable, yet it should also tell us something about the resistances that the various forms of the self-understanding of rock practitioners establish beyond the all-present violence of the dominant culture.

It would not be possible to run out of evidence that rock is **folk** music if this evidence were not somewhat suspicious precisely due to its abundance and immediate obviousness. Namely, who could believe, in the time of mass societies, that the masses still possess anything genuine – or, more precisely, it would be naïve to suppose that it is not in fact modern folkloric populism that supports what we saw as mass manipulation during the golden era of humanism in the 1960s – the manipulation whose subject we presupposed in one or another evil technocratic-bureaucracy. Now that the "techno" moment has disappeared from the map of social domination, it has become obvious that it is precisely the genuine folklore that constitutes a medium for voluntary servitude and that it is superfluous to ascribe any plans to the subject of domination, as the spontaneous idiocy of the master's discourse suffices for its rule, while the melodramatic confusion of its empirical agents is more likely a sign of how well they occupy their place in this discourse. One who expects the rulers to be coherent only wants to be ruled by a good emperor; whom one always already has by definition.

The sociological approach is therefore somewhat too limited, as it cannot explain the differences that we can somehow notice among the masses. If nothing else, this can already be seen from the ambivalent attitude of the representatives of power – in their genuine "love-hate relationship" with the so-called masses. Insofar as this entails the discourse of the master, we would definitely have grounds to seek the differences in the master-signifier, which "holds together" every master's discourse that brings together the masses as if on their material base; to therefore seek the difference in **what it is** that brings a variety of masses together. Naturally, it is true that this is achieved by anxiety; but it is too abstractly true to allow for any sort of differentiation.

Thus, if we have decided somewhat deductivistically yet trusting in the theory that supports us to seek differences among the masses that are brought together by the dispositive of the dominant discourses and the masses that gather, for example, at rock concerts, in the context of the master-signifier, then this, naturally, has nothing to do with any "semantic" contents of this designator. This stems already from the very concept of signifier: a signifier is differential, i.e. defined by its relationships with and differences from the other signifiers. Therefore, it is devoid of any "contents", but is instead defined by its distinguishing characteristics. This is true of the Saussurean signifier "in general" – and all the more so of the Lacanian master-signifier, but with additional subtleties that Saussure could not see simply because for him, the signifying field was **homogenous**. Precisely for this reason, he had to, naturally, ideologically presuppose the systemic nature of the linguistic system in advance – because, as we know today, the completeness of a system depends precisely on the non-homogeneity of the signifying field, i.e. on the fact that a system can only be complete and whole if it **does not** encompass all the signifiers, if it leaves out "at least one of them". The paradox that Saussure was unable to see is that a system is perfect precisely when it is not perfect – or, to put it less melo-dramatically: it is established by the function of exception or exclusion. This function is embodied in the master-signifier, S1; while semantics are only **derived** from this position. Initially, we there-fore cannot be interested in the "meaning", but rather in the **position**. Therefore we must explain the diversity of the masses – which are, naturally, always established by a certain "strategy" of the master-signifier – on the basis of, first and foremost, the position that the master-signifier establishes itself in.

However, in these efforts, we need to avoid simplifications, because we must not, by any means, presuppose that the ruling discourse (the discourse of the dominant culture) is necessarily the discourse of the master. Quite the reverse: social domination takes place as "patchwork" held together by the discourse of the ruling ideology – which has, in our time, supposedly already progressed from the archaisms of the pure master's discourse. One completely empirical reason is this: if it is characteristic of the current social present that it is "dominated" by the contradiction between the ruling ideology and the ideology of the rulers, then it is obvious that neither the former nor the latter can function as the master's discourse, because the contradiction could not exist in this case. The matrix of domination that somehow combines both contradictory elements of the current dominant culture must be capable of "encompassing" both components. This is something that the discourse of the master is "incapable of", precisely because it is **too strong**. If the master's discourse were indeed one of these two sides, it would have subjugated and eliminated the other side.

We will therefore address the issue gradually and begin with trivialities.

There is an evident difference between Pero Lovšin [frontman of punk band Pankrti] and every president of the Socialist Youth League: nobody knows the latter. Moreover, nobody would even recognise the latter if they met them in the street, even though – and herein lies the subtlety – both of them define the current situation in the street in their own ways. Naturally, this fact could lead to a conclusion regarding the complete replaceability of today's upstarts, and it would correspond to the abstract nature of the aforementioned difference, which is merely the difference between determinacy and indeterminacy. Simultaneously, such a conclusion would imply an erroneous supposition of the democratic nature of this governance. The dialectic of bureaucratic governance lies in the fact that replaceability by no means implies recallability and that replacements are subject to extremely strict conditions that, as we are being informed, severely restrict the personnel pool since this sort of replaceability also calls for **imperceptibility**. If the agents of domination are impossible to notice, then the alterations between them cannot be perceived either – just as our everyday experience proves. They ascribe to the old Asian wisdom, that the less the power holders are seen, the more their authority is felt.

At this point, our deliberation is becoming unpleasantly Hegelian – or, more precisely, it keeps steering into the waters of conventional conservative Hegelianism (the sort that is seen more as a fantasy of Hegel's opponents): we started with the question of the people, now we are discussing the authority; we were interested in the identity of folk musicians, but now rambling about the indistinguishable identity of the power holders has been forced upon us. Somehow we have slipped along the dialectical premise that "identity is non-

identity", that identity is defined by that which
is different from difference. However, we are still
holding on to materialistic theorisation, even to
the degree where we will not disappoint either the
materialist Hegel or our initial argumentation.

I am referring to the following: in asking ourselves about the identity of folk musicians, we
needed to raise the question of the difference that
defines this identity; and this is simply what we
tried to capture with the image of the power holders.
This "difference", however, turned out to be a non-
difference (everyone is replaceable). We will not use
the word shapelessness, otherwise any empirical
power holder could drag us through the courts, sub-
mitting proofs of their *carte d'identité*. However,
let us resort to a dialectical trick for the last time:
non-difference is, for example, the identicalness –
not the identicalness of any upstart, but rather of
the place they occupy, i.e. the locus of power. It
is clear that this place is defined tautologically and
with absolute identicalness, insofar as it is a decisive
place in the master's discourse, a master-signifier
that can be occupied exclusively or predominantly
by someone whose selection does not raise any
questions regarding the relationship between the
place where they are positioned, and the "element"
that is being positioned (this is a "personnel
condition" or, more concretely, a moral-political
qualification). The function therefore requires
someone who is imperceptible; or what will be
imperceptible is at least that the relationship
between the place and the *placed* can be problematic.
Already these two main variants provide ample

room for the constant empirical strategies of the discourse of power.

As we imagine ourselves to be materialists, we will hereby digress in the good Marxist spirit and ask ourselves what the general historical conditions for the possibility of our conceptualisation are. Attentive readers have most likely already guessed that we are discretely making use of Hegel's theory of monarchs as "idiots who dot the i's". After all, this conception is one of the privileged places in Hegel where Bataille's sentiment, "il ne savait pas comment il avait raison" ["s/he didn't know s/he was right"] applies: Hegel could not have known, either, as until this theory, Hegelian monarchs definitely had not existed (at least not in Europe); while after him, they were swiftly eliminated. Nonetheless, he produced a concept that explains all monarchic institutions, even if it does not literally apply to any of them. Hegel's concept of monarchs is a "rational abstraction" in the Marxist sense – and in his nastiness, Marx came very close to it when it dawned on him that monarchs were the appendages of their penises. However, Marx did not ask himself as he should, blinded for the grain of truth in the joke by the polemic spark: he did not ask himself why in the popular imagery, the penis is represented by a phallus.

After all, it is not so difficult to establish that no monarchy can successfully implement Hegel's concept, precisely insofar as it remains dedicated to the minimal naturalism of monarchic ontogenesis. This same ideological dispositive, whose signifying nature Hegel analysed so brilliantly, simultaneously

represents the absolute obstacle preventing the
realisation of Hegel's own concept: the nature of
the very concept of monarchs is such that due
to its internal immanent logic, it cannot realise
itself as a concept, but always merely through
ideological self-deception. This is how the practical
dimension of the ideological "lie" asserts itself in
a most obvious manner: the community must
believe in the natural genealogical determinacy of
monarchs in order for their unnatural signifying
"nature" to realise itself at all. Or more generally:
the very cultural concept of "nature" is such that
it cannot be conceived as an ideological concept
conveyed through culture; "nature" is inherent to
"culture" precisely in the sense that it (culturally)
manifests itself as external to culture. Precisely
according to this fictitiousness, nature belongs
to culture as a **cultural**, i.e. ideological, concept.
After all, this is amply demonstrated by the history
of ideologies: when "philosophers" start doubting
the natural determinacy of a ruler, their first and
most spontaneous gesture is to proclaim them as an
"anti-natural" phenomenon, a monster and tyrant –
and start inciting a revolution. In fact, only in this
manner, is thinking in the context of the "nature/
culture" opposition completed, and we must not
forget that this is bourgeois thinking. Hence: either
the question of "nature-culture" is not raised at all
with regard to monarchs and monarchs are in fact
"beneath" their concept; or the question is indeed
raised, but the monarchs are thus, in reality,
abolished. History misses (its) concept in any case.
In reality, monarchs only exist insofar as they

are not conceptualised; but as soon as conceptualisation is possible, they are already gone.

The heroism of theory lives through the lapses of history.

During their Marxist phases, Močnik and Žižek established the concept of post-revolutionary socialist bureaucracy, which generally occupies the place of the absent ruling class as the representative of the proletariat (see preface to the miscellany **Psihoanaliza in kultura**, DZS, 1981). This could lead us to the conclusion that bureaucratic discourse is the master's discourse "in general", as Močnik in fact hints in his article '*Stalinizem danes*' (*Naši razgledi*, 25 September 1981). However, paradoxically, in another yet simultaneously published text, which apparently focuses on orthodox Lacanianism, the same author builds on the conclusion that "Stalinist" discourse is the university discourse, i.e. a discourse of knowledge (see 'sub pluribus unum', *Problemi* 209–211, 1981). Inconsistency, the turning point between the Marxist and Lacanian phase – or something worse?

Neither – and to avoid beating around the bush, let us put it straight: by becoming the discourse of the master "in general", the master's discourse, as a rule, progresses to the university discourse. In the master's discourse, the agent is S1, i.e. the master signifier; while S2, i.e. the signifying battery of knowledge ("held together" by S1) is positioned in the place of the other (for more information about the matrix of the four discourses and a few commentaries, see miscellany **Gospostvo, vzgoja, analiza: zbornik tekstov Lacanove šole**

psihoanalize *[Dominance, education, analysis: an anthology of Lacanian school of psychoanalysis]*, Analecta, DDU Univerzum, Ljubljana 1983). In the field of Marx's criticism of the Hegelian philosophy of state law, the difference between S1 and S2 is the difference between the monarchic function (i.e. literally the "dot on the i") and the knowledge of counsellors, ministers, chancellors, etc. The truth of this difference is the split subject S – i.e., in Marx's lucid diction, precisely the empirical monarch as an appendage of his penis. The product of this classification is a surplus enjoyment, for instance the surplus and "unnecessary", supplementary enjoyment that the empirical subject of the monarchic function has due to his statehood propagation activity. Because, according to the logic of desire, this necessarily places him in relationship with death (if anyone is a "being-for-death", then this is precisely the Hegelian monarch), his only function in life is to father a descendant, i.e. to put his own death in order. Of course, this gains a witty historical class interpretation with the revolution, as the guillotine realises the concept of the monarch, so to speak. However, more than plebeian interpretative humour underlies the historical realisation under the guillotine's blade: this realisation must be taken **literally**, and as we have already stated, the realisation of the concept of the monarch represents the end (historical as well as conceptual) of the monarch and monarchy. This is the final range of the monarchic S1: when the guillotine severs the historical class **concept** together with the empirical natural king's head.

Therefore, not every regicide is a revolution – and the assassination attempt by Damiens is symptomatic in this sense: Damiens attempted to assassinate Louis XV because he saw him as a usurper. However, for him, the usurper was this concrete, empirical, naturally distinct Louis Capet: unlike Saint-Just, he did not yet see that the king is a usurper due to his "kingness", i.e. regardless of the subtleties of hereditary law. This, however, does not lead Saint-Just – and herein lies his greatness – to the false conclusion that Louis Capet "is not guilty of anything": quite the opposite, he is guilty, even though he has, in a sense, "nothing to do" with the matter. S1 is impossible to eliminate in any other way, but to eliminate the natural empirical individual that subjectivises himself through it: in this manner, we do him the final justice, grant him the highest and ultimate recognition that belongs to him in accordance with his own concept.

Why? Because this very disproportion between the empirical individual who is, after all, naturally abstract, and the concrete generality of the concept that we can reach through this **inadequate** abstract individuality, affirms, in the highest degree, the **irreducible heterogeneity** of the master-signifier, S1. The whole scheme of the master's discourse depends on the irreducibility of the difference between the master-signifier S1 and the signifying battery of "all other" S2 signifiers and is based on this irreducibility. Precisely for this reason, it is crucial that in the case of monarchs, this irreducible heterogeneous natural moment – filiation, blood, lineage – intervenes. This regressiveness of the monarch is the "driving force" that enables the master's discourse; which is extremely dramatic, if we consider the post-revolutionary autocrats that in fact **lack** the foundation for S1 – insofar as it needs to be **irrational** in accordance with its own concept. Napoleon was a master – but he was a poor master precisely because he was **qualified** to be one: he was a good general, a capable official, and his domination was **motivated**, which means that it cannot qualify as S1 irreducible-unmotivated, as the concept of domination demands. Napoleon's Waterloo stemmed from the fact that he was too good of a commander: what had made him rise up also tore him down. The mythologies claiming that, in case of Waterloo, he was defeated due to the mud that got in the way of the wheels of his cannons and that he struggled at the Berezina River because he had a cold, attempt to pay him an undeserved tribute retroactively: that he would at least fall in accordance with an irrational logic if he arose by his own merit. Mussolini was closer to the old masters: he would have his photographs taken as an aviator, a swimmer, and a reaper: he knew – and acted accordingly – that tyrants entered history **in white stockings**. Especially in the 20th century, this style fared better – and confirmed that the element of **impurity**, inconsistency, and particularity is precisely what provides the master's discourse with its purity, power, and general validity.

This particular residual alibi, where S1 needs to remain, is lost precisely with the "generalisation" of the master's discourse in Stalinism, precisely with its elevation to the discourse of the master "in general". In the place of the agent, it is replaced by S2, the signifying battery of knowledge. S1 slips to the position of the truth; and in the Stalinist discourse, this truth may always show itself only as a concealed and unattainable surplus, additional – yet decisive and qualifying – **knowledge**. The Stalinist discourse is not a "university discourse" because it would be any "better, more scientific, etc." as the previous master's discourses – but because it functions in the name of knowledge and represents the foundations for another knowledge, a certain knowledge in another place. This "other knowledge", this knowledge "elsewhere" (in the place of the truth) does not operate through its contents, but rather through its position. The "something more" that the Stalinist master supposedly knows – or, to put it more precisely: whose depository the Stalinist institutions are – is nothing "substantive", it is in fact "nothing" (whenever we get our hands on these secret archives, we are always disappointed in their contents). It is merely a signifier positioned in another place. It is S1 below the line, in the place of the truth. In Stalinism, the secret police or the political police operates strictly with its form: it does not know anything more, its function is in the secrecy of its knowledge. Whatever the Stalinist secret state police drags into the light (in indictments at judicial processes, newspaper editorials, statements of the highest bodies, etc.) usually turns out to be a patchwork of unverified or fabricated gossip, insinuations, malicious rumours, poorly-founded and worst possible interpretations, and so on: yet **all of this**

functions precisely due to its incompleteness.
It functions by being unproven, baseless, poorly
constructed, etc. – which conveys an impression
that **there is something more behind it**. In
Stalinism, domination is driven precisely by the
assumption that there is something more behind
everything – a pure form of secret knowledge. In its
very concept, Stalinism is therefore domination
based on the secret police. Meanwhile, in Stalinism,
people's wisdom – that statehood-enabling mass
stupidity – functions precisely in this manner and
exposes the mechanism in its irrationality: "We
know that all these accusations are baseless", the
loyal citizens will tell you, "but they wouldn't drag
this guy into the court if something wasn't behind it".

We have made this digression through the
theory of the former and current forms of domination because of the question of the specific
difference of the masses as they are established by
the mass culture in today's **progressive** (rock, punk)
variant. We are no longer discussing mass culture
"in general", as the internal class division of mass
culture is nowadays already a self-evident fact –
self-evident in the sense that the fronts cannot be
overlooked, and that the class struggle in the field
of mass culture has already been developed well
enough to attain self-awareness. It is enough to take
a look at the Ljubljana television or radio station to
see how that side is very well aware of this struggle –
and how it organises itself in it consciously.

We will get our answer if we apply the des-
criptive findings from the first part of this text
to the theoretical context of its second part: the

identification strategy of the subversion of the ruling ideologies and the ideologies of the rulers is only possible when **based** on the fact that nobody considers, even for a second, that this could be the real, true discourse of power. Identification is therefore only possible based on the absolute difference as established by the context of the "mass cultural" (if we stated "artistic", we would need to resort to double quotation marks) event.

This digression through theory has now brought us even too far back, and we have seemingly ended up in a tautology: we asked ourselves about the constitution of the masses in this mass culture, and now we are establishing that such a constitution is only possible on the basis of the "mass culture". Does this mass culture therefore represent "its own foundation"? The tautology is merely apparent: it is that the identification subversion is only possible based on a certain – to put it conditionally – artistic-cultural context. This context **is indeed** "its own foundation" insofar it participates in the ideology of **autonomous art**; insofar it therefore participates in the modern concept of art. (The "modern" ideological concept of art has been conceptualised in the text "*Zgodovinski materializem pred vprašanjem 'umetnost in družba'*" in: A. Hauser. **Umetnost in družba**, DZS 1980: modern artistic practices are those that are ideologically based on art itself as well as on their own ideology.)

This, however, is merely less than half of the answer: what we especially need to explain is how the progressive practice of mass culture participates in the ideology of art autonomy. This explanation is all the more crucial because nowadays, after all, the autonomist art ideology is one of the fundamental components of the ruling cultural ideology (and therefore also one of the main bases for the strategy of the cultural bureaucracy). That autonomist ideology has a different role in the progressive mass cultural practices than in the ruling cultural ideology, is directly obvious already from the fact that the ruling cultural ideology perceives and presents itself as something apolitical (they are "above" politics), while the progressive mass culture practices are explicitly **politicised**. The historical contribution of today's mass culture practices – that in which they are different from the previous eras in "art history" – is simultaneously the element through which these practices establish their **class position**: the element of its opposition to the cultural-ideological practices on the horizon of the dominant culture. With a simple formula, this "contribution" – i.e., this class position – can be summed up as follows: **in today's progressive mass cultural activities, the opposition between "art" and "politics"**, which is the fundamental ideological presupposition in the ideology of art autonomism, **is transferred to the "art" practices themselves**. This transfer thoroughly shakes up the ideological concept of "art" while simultaneously undermining the very ideological opposition between "art" and "politics".

This has nothing to do with any principled declarations of the orthodox or leftist type ("all arts are political") or academic-conservative prattling ("even politics is art"). Instead, it is

a practical subversion in a historically-established
ideological field (thus, in a sense, in the opponent's
field, and doubly so: in the field of traditional autonomist ideology **and** in the field of mass culture,
dominated by the ideological apparatuses of the state,
i.e. radio, television, producers of phonograms,
event organisers, cultural and congress centres, etc.).
After almost two decades of regressions and obscurantist renewals, the problem posed by the autonomist avant-garde in the 1960s (OHO) – which
the *Katalog*[3] publication attempted to solve in 1968
and was, naturally, unable to solve it due to
its entrapment into the elitist marginality and
because of the context of the spontaneity of
contemporaneous mass movements – is therefore
finally being solved. (The *Katalog* publication should
be credited for swiftly realising and admitting its
failure – and thus opening the path towards the
theoretisation of the issue, towards the theoretical
production that has largely contributed to the
production of today's historical constellation.)

In the very "artistic" practice, the ideological
opposition "art vs politics" starts functioning
as a **formal-structural principle** that ensures the
heterogeneity of the signifying field, as well as,
concretely, the **difference** between S1 (a healing
master-signifier, a "filler", a "patch", etc.) and
S2 (a signifying battery of "all" other signifiers).
This is the most general formula that we can use
to encompass today's progressive mass culture

---

3   OHO was a conceptual art and concrete poetry collective from
       Slovenia. *Katalog* was the special issue of *Problemi* journal edited
       by OHO members in 1968.

practices, but it is also an abstract formula insofar as it only brings the principle that **has yet to be produced** through the concrete manipulations of this heterogeneity. However, already from this purely abstract and principled definition we can see why it is precisely this strategy that is so subversive in particular for the Stalinist ("university") practice of domination: the Stalinist discourse practice is based precisely on concealing the difference between S1 and S2 – by operating through S2, while it actively represses, conceals, and stifles the S1 in the place of the truth. The "artistic" staging of the heterogeneity between S1 and S2 therefore has a "demystifying" impact on the Stalinist discourse: it allows for a genuine, naive "art" pleasure (because it practices a naive enlightened – demystifying – "critique of the ideology") and shows the Stalinist discourse for "what it is": the discourse of domination, sub specie of the master's discourse. It reduces the Stalinist discourse to its "transcendental matrix": i.e., precisely to the master's discourse as a **condition for the possibility** of the university discourse. Of course, from the theoretical viewpoint, this mystifying subversion is naive and "too limited" – yet it is nevertheless effective in practice: naturally, more so because of the very object of its demystification rather than because of its own naive gesture. As it is, the university discourse of domination is, due to its own structure, **specifically vulnerable** to the criticism that ("wrongfully") unmasks it as the discourse of the master.

Of course, such critical success also represents the greatest danger for the mass cultural practices:

on the one hand, it pushes them into the globalist critique of domination, which is blind precisely for the historical and structural specifics (i.e., for the very **class** nature) of the various ideological mechanisms of domination; while on the other hand, it pushes them into the correlative valorisation of the "cultural-artistic" autonomy in contrast to the ideologically-politically dirty empirics. Mass cultural practices thus succumb to classic anarchism on the one hand, and cultural obscurantism on the other hand: after all, it is precisely this bizarre anarchic obscurantist slush that is most characteristic of the spontaneous ideology of punk and rock practitioners. However paradoxical this may seem, the greatest danger that threatens the progressive practitioners of mass culture is that they could couple with the bureaucratic elite in the dominant traditional culture. As it happens, right at this moment, this elite is experiencing development in the other direction: due to the progressive Stalinisation of the political bureaucratic "elite", the non-antagonistic contradictions between the cultural and political rulers are intensifying; and the elites that get their power from the ideology of art autonomism, "anti-totalitarian" anarchism is, in such a situation, simply the handiest ideological cliche.

The structure of progressive mass cultural practices is therefore incredibly entertaining and places theoretical reflection into a productively paradoxical position: on the one hand, we are forced to resort to the "classic" concepts from the traditional ideological junk room (e.g. art, politics, autonomy, etc.); while on the other hand, these concepts have always already been subverted in the mass-cultural practices, and we should therefore constantly use them in quotation marks. The only way to write about these practices therefore lies precisely in the abandonment of the quotation marks, i.e. the self-satisfied intellectualist distance – and in practising some sort of a **punk theory**, which is precisely the materialist theory of the last ten years with its Maoist lunacy **subsequently** turns out to be. This must lead us to the conclusion that the theory of these practices is always already being written, insofar as it is materialist theory – that we are therefore experiencing one of the privileged historical moments when reality has ascended to the level of theory, i.e. its concept. Naturally, in this regard, the encounter between theoretical practices and "practical" practices, theory and art, progressive intelligentsia and the working masses is completely and thoroughly erroneous: namely, artistic practices attain the theoretical level precisely with what is **not** theoretical about them, while theory is on par with them – not because of its theoretical dimensions, but in the sense of its **style**, i.e. its artistic component. This also means that the nature of the conceptual error is **different** on both sides: art is politicised and theorised through its artistry; while theory reaches its counterpart precisely through the moment of its inherent otherness. This once again leads to the conclusion that theory preserves its dominant role in practice – especially in the practice of the class struggle.

What makes progressive mass-cultural practices art practices is precisely what makes them political practices as well; and what makes them art practices

is, for example, the reason why they are not theory –
i.e., their theoretical insufficiency, deficiency. Their
political nature therefore results from their theoretical naivety, while their theoretical-political potential
depends precisely on their non-theoretical artistry.
However, as the theoretical-political potential is what
makes these practices art, they are thus art practices
precisely insofar as they are not art.

Q. E. D. [quod erat demonstrandum/thus it
has been demonstrated]

Thus, we have only somewhat more logistically
demonstrated what we have already recorded at
the level of description: that identification is only
possible based on it not being sameness. We are
therefore merely referring to the strategies of producing and explicating the **heterogeneity** of the
signifying field. These strategies vary (for the catalogue, see the first part of this text, where we have
divided them according to the object of identification; here we will analyse them in view of the
structure of the identification process – which
simultaneously already **prejudices** the object of
identification, as the various strategies of hetero-
genization literally produce various points of
identification).

We can say that these strategies can be divided
into two extremes: **"unreserved" identification**,
where heterogeneity is excluded from the practised
discourse; and **"ironic" identification**, where
heterogeneity operates within the discourse itself.
Unreserved identification does not only appear to
be more radical, but is also radically borderline, and
therefore it seems as if it represents the concept

of all possible strategies. In this light, "ironic" identification still seems to be traditionalist and intellectualistic. Although this interpretation has its advantages – it is, by all means, crucial as the first analytical step, as it offers the key for "decoding" – we find it overly purist and radical and therefore ultimately reductionist.

Let us therefore take a look at the "ironic" identification, which is, in our opinion, illustrated by the band **Pankrti**. Especially in case of the song *"Dolgcajt"*, the immediate impression is the erroneous experience of heterogeneity between S1 and S2 – at the completely formal level, that interpellates the listeners to an alienating **veil** through which they constitute themselves as subjects (for the concept of alienation, see J. Lacan. *Štirje temeljni koncepti psihoanalize*, CZ 1980). Initially, we face a choice: we can listen to either the music or the lyrics. If we listen to the music, we do not hear the lyrics; and if we want to understand the lyrics, we do not hear the music, but also fail to understand the lyrics. **Precisely in this manner**, the "lyrics", i.e. the verbal signifier, constitutes itself as S1, i.e. a signifier without the signified; but it is precisely in this manner that it "bestows meaning" on the entire signifying chain – the only difference being that there is no "signifying chain", because the "second signifier" is massively represented with the musical mass that "we do not hear". Our prize is therefore merely formal: we have acquired S1, yet lost "everything", i.e., everything **plus** S1, which is "nothing" without what it is supposed to constitute according to its function. However, the listeners are stubborn: therefore they will resort to a solution made possible by the specific medium of phonograms (the technological-mythological moment!) and will listen **repeatedly**. Then, perhaps, they will eventually comprehend the words after all; and what will they comprehend? Nothing else but the **repetition of stereotypes** (political slogans or expressive-sentimental cliches). This means that at the level of semantics, the listeners will reacquire what they needed to do at the level of pragmatics in order to reach semantics at all – namely, the pure **mechanism of repetition**.

We keep moving within a certain art-political ideology, and never actually depart from it – yet the ideology runs "idle", i.e. its mechanism is exposed and is therefore **subverted** already in this manner.

At the precise moment where we therefore reach the "true nature" of the verbal signifier – which is, at least in the context of phonocentric ideology, privileged in its performance of the S1 function – we have already lost it, as it has started to function as a "message", i.e. as S2. We can reach S1 as the forced repetition of a meaningless stereotype only when we "interpret" it as S2, as a "message", even if it is meaningless. In this moment, S1 functions as the musical dimension – insofar as we **do not listen** to it.

The ironic distance therefore does not lie in the distance towards the "message" and is not based on a sort of a surplus knowledge, etc. Instead, it is merely the distance between S1 and S2 in its irreducibility and **pure form**. Or, to put it more precisely: if in the case of *Pankrti* we can refer to a sort of an intellectual distance and irony that occasionally reminds us of traditional ironic strategies, the **pure horizontal signifying operation** is nevertheless the material basis for this enlightenment effect: the only thing that is produced is the (horizontal) heterogeneity between S1 and S2 – therefore blocking the possibility for any meta-locutionary position that classic irony is based on already in advance.

The horizontal nature of this operation means precisely that S1 operates on the same plane as S2 – that S1 is therefore elevated from its position below the line, where it is pushed to by the Stalinist discourse of domination "through knowledge". Therefore the practice of *Pankrti* is, in its formal structure (and not because of any "substantive message" – we could even say despite any potential messages), a **politically anti-Stalinist** practice.

In this light, the unreserved identification in the likes of the group *Laibach* appears as a reduction of the signifying heterogeneity to the repeating stereotypy of the S1 signifier – which is why this practice (unlike in the case of *Pankrti*) can encompass "all" art "forms" without any reservations or differences. Paradoxically, however, what sounds the most "artistically convincing" is precisely what establishes this entirety of artistic genres, yet itself is not art: this group's programme manifests it. If in the case of *Pankrti* the dangerous line was in enlightened intellectualism, in the case of *Laibach* this same line of degeneration lies in the psychotic ritual: insofar the group focuses on the unreserved repetition of the bare S1, their own practice in all of its repetitive stereotypy starts to function as S2 that lacks S1 – where the possibility for symbolisation is missing. Or, to put it more simply: if the position of *Pankrti* threatens to slip into passive harmonious artistry, the position of *Laibach* threatens to succumb to unhinged activism.

We do not mention the "dangers" that threaten both of these extreme formulations in progressive mass culture because we wish to wag a finger and preach, but because this "line of degeneration" constitutes an **internal structural moment** of both practices. This is the darker side of the constitutive contradiction of today's alternative as we formulated it in the first part of the present text. The degree to which this internal contradiction is constitutive of alternative practices – insofar as it is an **historical** contradiction that connects these practices with the historical context and insofar as this historical context is established by the domination of dominant culture – is the degree to which the internal contradiction in the alternative is the **trace** of the domination of dominant culture that opposes, it as well as the degree to which the alternative practice itself is characterised by the domination against which it revolts.

The "correct" strategy therefore does not lie in the declarative abolishment (let alone the "overcoming") of the constitutive contradiction, but rather in its preservation: its "manipulation". This strategy, however, is not possible without at least minimal theoretical foundations, which the present text also seeks to establish.

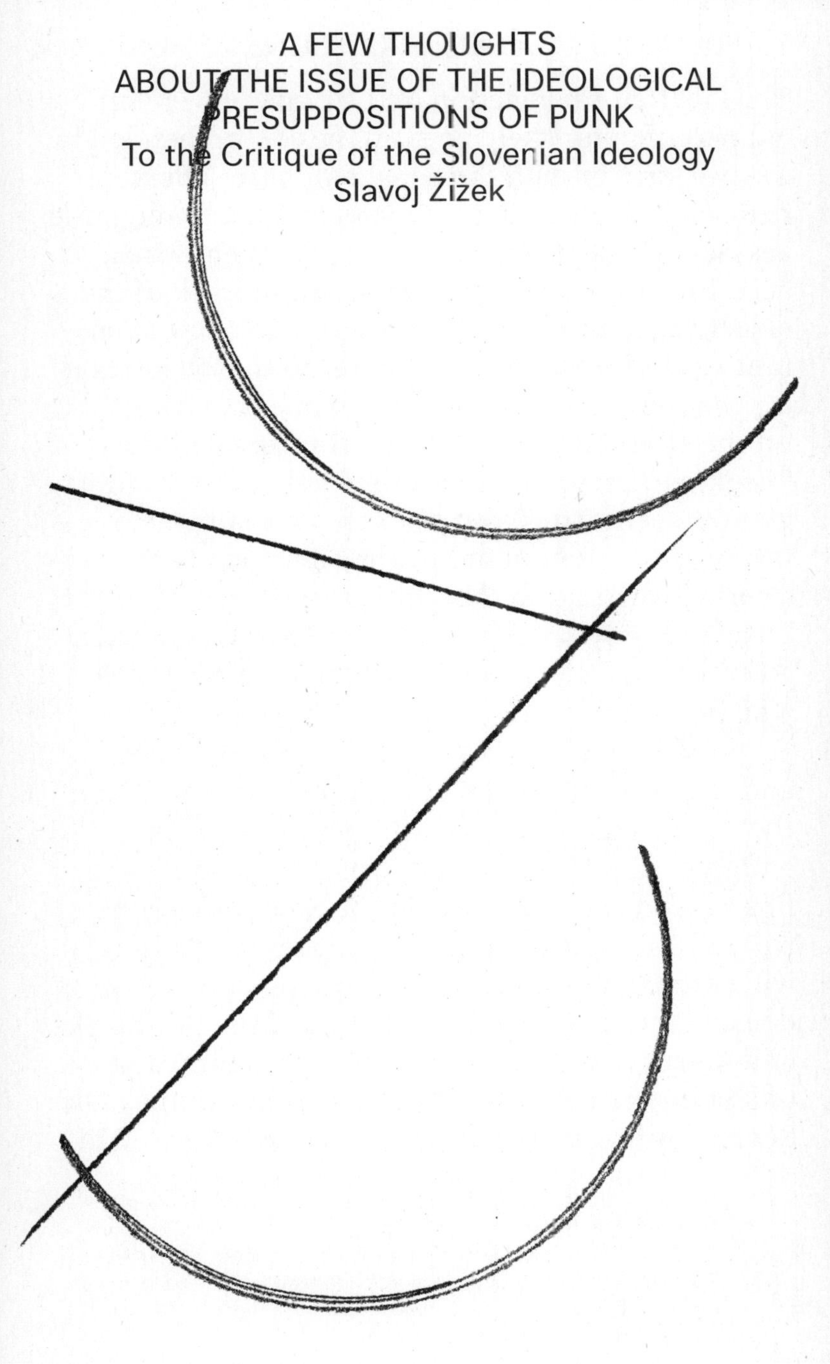

A FEW THOUGHTS
ABOUT THE ISSUE OF THE IDEOLOGICAL
PRESUPPOSITIONS OF PUNK
To the Critique of the Slovenian Ideology
Slavoj Žižek

The fact that the reaction to the punk movement is a part of punk itself[1] needs to be comprehended in a sense stricter than the usual emphases characteristic of particular phenomenological and avant-garde aesthetics, claiming that it is the recipient whose active reception fills the empty framework of the objective features of an artwork with concrete substantive contents. We come closer to this by looking at the type of jokes whose punch lines are based on the characteristic dialectical reversal of the "negative" into "positive": precisely what, at first glance, seems to be the problem or an obstacle is in fact the denouement, the solution. There is a certain reputation that Jews from Central and Eastern Europe, in particular, are masters of such jokes, so let us take a look at an example of a Jewish joke from the Soviet Union:

Rabinovich comes to the emigration office and wants to submit an emigration request. When the surprised official asks him why he wishes to emigrate, Rabinovich says: "For two reasons. The first reason is that I'm afraid the Soviet government will fall and that the rightist counter-revolution will come to power, and it will, just like it always does, blame us Jews for all the sins of the Bolsheviks and once again persecute us..." The astonished official interrupts him: "But that's impossible! The Soviet government is so solid that it will never fall!"

1   The text is a reworked fragment of the research paper 'Vloga nezavednih fantazem v procesu oblikovanja identitete Slovencev' (The Role of Unconscious Phantasms in the Process of Forming Slovenian Identity), taking place at the Institute of Sociology in the framework of the project on the processes of the formation of the identity of Slovenians, financed by the RSS.

Rabinovich continues calmly: "Well, and that's the second reason!"

What is essential for us is the immanent dialogic nature of this joke: if Rabinovich simply listed both reasons for wanting to emigrate, this would be nothing but contradictory nonsense. All the charm and punch line of the joke is that the very argument against the first reason turns out to be the second reason. It is also superfluous to note that the only real reason is the second reason, i.e. that the only reason for listing the first reason is, in the literal sense, provocative: it is merely stated so that it provokes the other speaker into asking a question that leads directly to the second, true reason.

Our starting supposition would therefore be that the logic of the so-called "punk provocation" is precisely the same: the immediacy of punk performance itself plays the role of the "first reason", which is supposed to provoke our reaction, through which we can grasp the actual reason behind the performance. Let us try to explain this logic with an example that has recently stirred up the Slovenian public quite a bit: the appearance of the group Laibach in a weekly TV show on Ljubljana television. The performance has provoked two main types of reactions. The first, characteristic especially of the so-called "general public", is summed up nicely already with the title and subtitle of the article dedicated to this event in the *Nedeljski dnevnik* newspaper of 3 July 1983: "Five young men reminisce about the infamous painter / Who has made the shirts for "Laibach" / (p. 4) – in short, the performance is perceived as direct flirting with

Nazism, as a semi-concealed revival of a sort of a proto-Nazi, totalitarian ideological stance. However, what is much more interesting for us is the reaction of those people – in particular the socio-political forums as well as quite a few "open", "critical" intellectuals – who are completely aware of the senselessness of the reproach that Laibach is a Nazi group, yet are nevertheless profoundly bothered by something about their performance: an unease that is usually expressed with the words "apathy", "depersonalisation", "dehumanisation", and the like. For example, let us take a look at the standpoint of the Presidency of the ZSMS (Socialist Youth League of Slovenia):

> "The ZSMS rejects the manner of social criticism employed, for example, by the group 'Laibach', which, apart from anarchism, also brings apathy, while emphasising that this is not a sort of a Nazi group as depicted by the administrative attitude to the youth culture" (*Delo*, 8 July 1983, p. 2).

The standpoint of the MK SZDL Ljubljana (Socialist Alliance of Working People) was similar, though somewhat more severe:

> "The concept of the performers – to allegedly underline the alienation of the political authority with expressions of totalitarianism (their symbols function as a strong allusion to Nazi-fascism, Stalinism, etc.) – is by no means acceptable. Any critique of negative social phenomena should be severe, realistic, and uncompromising, yet devoid

of the anarchic apathy and depersonalisation, which is not and should not be characteristic of our socialist self-management society. For this reason, the Presidency of the MK SZDL Ljubljana – while underlining the dehumanised expression that is, in an intensified form, characteristic of the group Laibach and which irritates with clear allusions to Nazi-fascism – resolutely rejects such activities of this group and protests against them" (*Ljubljanski dnevnik*, 30 June 1983, p. 5).

If we set aside how badly the MK SZDL truly wishes to hear any "severe" and "uncompromising" criticism of social phenomena, we are left with the basic fact that both of these organisations are not bothered by criticism in itself, but rather in particular by the position of "apathy" and "depersonalisation" from which it is expressed. Instead of pointing out the contradictions and negative sides of our society in an insightful, witty, and ironic manner, Laibach offers individuals who recite the acquired totalitarian formulas "like machines". In short, instead of a vivacious spirit, they offer dead letters. We have thus touched upon the central problem of the ideological reproduction, which, insofar as we remain within a specific ideological field, necessarily remains hidden to us: i.e., the fact that a particular ideology at the level of the subjective economy of the individuals that are subject to it, by no means reproduces itself through its argumentative power, but rather through the dimension which Pascal, who was perhaps the first to identify it, named the "machine" or the "automaton", and which has nowadays been developed first and foremost by Louis Althusser in his theory of "ideological state apparatuses": ideology is not an "illusion" floating in the air. Instead, it is very much "material" and involves a whole range of material practices. As Pascal emphasises, this "custom" "makes so many men Christians; custom that makes them Turks, heathens, artisans, soldiers, etc." (*Pensées*, 252) and – as we could add – agents of self-management. The key element at this point is Pascal's famous fragment about the necessity of the wager (*Pensées*, 233): the first, longer part of the fragment takes place at the level of proving that "betting that God exists" is justified. However, the argument breaks down as Pascal's partner in the dialogue makes the following claim that transfers the discussion to a completely different level:

"…'Yes, but I have my hands tied and my mouth closed; I am forced to wager, and am not free. I am not released, and am so made that I cannot believe. What, then, would you have me do?' True. But at least learn your inability to believe, since reason brings you to this, and yet you cannot believe. Endeavour then to convince yourself, not by increase of proofs of God, but by the abatement of your passions. You would like to attain faith, and do not know the way; you would like to cure yourself of unbelief, and ask the remedy for it. Learn of those who have been bound like you, and who now stake all their possessions. These are people who know the way which you would follow, and who are cured of an ill of which you would be cured. Follow the way by which they began; by acting as if they believed, taking the holy water, having masses said, etc. Even this will naturally make you believe, and deaden your acuteness.

...

Now, what harm will befall you in taking this side? You will be faithful, humble, grateful, generous, a sincere friend, truthful. Certainly you will not have those poisonous pleasures, glory and luxury; but will you not have others? I will tell you that you will thereby gain in this life, and that, at each step you take on this road, you will see so great certainty of gain, so much nothingness in what you risk, that you will at last recognise that you have wagered for something certain and infinite, for which you have given nothing."

Pascal's final answer is therefore as follows: abandon rational argumentation and subject yourself to the ideological ritual, act *as if* you had faith, and faith will come on its own. That this argumentation is not reserved only for the Catholic faith, but is instead relevant for the ideological process in general, is, after all, confirmed by the fact that referring to the issue of Pascal's wager was once very popular among the French communists. The Marxist version of Pascal goes something like this: a bourgeois intellectual has his hands tied and his mouth closed. He appears to be free, bound only by the arguments of his reason, but is in fact pervaded with bourgeois prejudices. These preconceptions do not let go of him, and therefore he cannot believe in the meaning of history, in the historical mission of the working class. What should he do, then? The answer: first, he should at least realise that he is unable to believe in the meaning of history: even though reason brings him to the fact that the working class is the holder of historical meaning, he is nevertheless such that he cannot believe. Therefore, he should not endeavour to prove the truth of the working class's historical mission, but rather focus on keeping his petty-bourgeois passions and prejudices in check. He should learn from those who had been as powerless as he but who are now ready to risk everything for the Revolution. He should follow the way in which they began: by acting as if they believed in the mission of the working class, being active in the Party, promoting the workers' movement, gathering aid for those on strike, etc. In time, this has completely naturally resulted in personal faith as well. Now, what harm has befallen them for deciding for this, although they had not believed? They have become loyal, humble, selfless, noble, and committed. Indeed, they have had to give up certain rotten pleasures of the petty bourgeoisie, egocentric intellectualistic toying, etc.; but they have instead – regardless of the honesty of their wager regarding the meaning of history – gained so much until today: they live a full and meaningful life, and all their activities are permeated by the awareness that they are making their modest contribution to a great and noble mission... This trap is certainly very effective, as it allows intellectuals to give up critical thinking in good faith that they are thus merely abandoning their egocentric individualism and contributing to a great and noble cause.

When it comes to this "custom", though, one needs to be careful, as it is a direct invitation to an erroneous understanding in the style of referring to a "power of habit", etc. However, what is hidden behind this "custom" is, in fact, a so-called performative dimension of the ideological ritual, i.e. that through its practising, the ritual in itself establishes the symbolic reality that it is referring to. This "performative" dimension of ideological discourse is perhaps easiest to approach through a certain everyday "psychological experience" that is known well enough to any at least somewhat refined observer of the human nature: let us take a look at an example of a problematic interpersonal relationship, in which one party in the relationship has committed some extremely inappropriate act. The atmosphere is tense: everyone knows what this individual has done, and everyone knows that everyone else knows this. Let us suppose that somebody finally makes a decision and solves this situation by stating what they all knew: thus, the entire inter-subjective relationship changes at once, as everyone needs to acknowledge this statement and can no longer act as if they do not know. What is essential here is that the one that finally states the issue and thus releases the tension does not say anything new: strictly speaking, the informational value of their message equals nothing, as everyone not only knew already, but they even knew that everyone else knew. This sort of statement is – perhaps more than what are nowadays already worn-out examples like "I promise to attend!", "I am hereby opening this meeting!", "I hereby name this ship 'Joseph Stalin'", etc. – a pure example of a performative, although it is a constative in its form (pure information about a particular fact, e.g. "You have cheated us.", "You have been stealing"). Such a statement puts an end to the entire previous network of intersubjective relationships that was based precisely on a sort of a symbolic suspension of this fact – even though everyone knew, they acted as if they did not know, while the symbolic "effectiveness" of their knowing was somehow put in parentheses. Such a statement is, therefore, a pure example of an intervention of a signifier as such: because at the level of the signified, it is entirely redundant and therefore superfluous, if we perceive speech as a means of expression, communicating information, emotions, etc.

On these foundations, we can also easily explain a specific type of intellectual conformism, characteristic of real socialism, when, for example, in case of some severe administrative or police intervention of the authorities, the following argumentation takes place: "We all know that this is outrageous, but why keep talking about it when we can achieve nothing except complicate the situation further". The truth is, of course, that merely publicly stating what "everyone already knows and what they know everyone knows" would be very much explosive indeed, as the system reproduces itself precisely by people not discussing things that "everyone knows". There are situations where the most subversive thing to do is to thoroughly naively state the obvious fact that "the king is naked".[2]

Such an intellectual distance – where an individual "is well aware of the facts", and yet they still

 SLAVOJ ŽIŽEK

take part in the symbolic ritual of the ruling ideology – is perhaps the purest example of how a certain ideology keeps us at the level of "machines" precisely when we believe "our spirit is free". On the personal level, we are convinced that this is merely an "external mask"; yet the degree to which this "mask" in fact exerts its control upon us is attested to precisely by the catastrophic consequences of somebody questioning it and stating that the king is naked.

To the subjects/subordinates of a particular ideology, the fact that this ideology is rooted in "customs", in its own material ritual, appears, "from the inside", as its "mystic", "irrational" feature, as its boundless tautological facticity: the law is the law because it is the law; ultimately, we need to obey it because it is the law rather than because it is good, just, and so on. This fact has been observed by many of the most insightful theologians, e.g. Kierkegaard, who knew very well that the statement, "I believe in

2   This, perhaps, goes to show that words are not the only way to escape actions (in the sense of the infamous phrase "let's put our money where our mouth is" or "actions speak louder than words"), but that in certain circumstances, actions can represent an escape from the word: the true word, the one that would make it impossible for the existing situation to continue. From this perspective, the ordinary proclamation contained in almost every statement of the socio-political forums in Slovenia – i.e., the variation on the topic "rather than focusing on empty declarations, conclusions, and words, let us take action: people expect actions from us, not merely empty words", the variation that has almost become a trademark or a distinguishing characteristic of bureaucrats – attains the characteristics of what we, in the psychoanalytic theory, refer to as acting out: retreating into activity in order to avoid the symbolic resolution of a specific tense situation. The answer to the ruling powers must therefore be: stop acting and start talking, you have worked long enough, done whatever you wanted to do, but now it is time that you spoke – i.e., utter the word that will not be "empty", the word that will stop you from continuing to do what you have been doing.

Christ because he is wise and just" is a horrible blasphemy – in reality, the relationship is quite the opposite: only based on my faith in him, does Christ appear to me in all his wisdom and goodness! Naturally, the naive enlightened critique can only perceive such a standpoint as an example of extreme dogmatic delusion, blind subjugation to authority; while we, if we stem from the thesis about the primacy of the "ideological state apparatuses", soon see its hidden "materialistic core": the symbolic ideological ritual is far from being merely an "external expression" of internal faith, something that is, in the last instance, non-essential and secondary. Instead, it is constitutive for internal faith, as the path to true faith leads merely through the "machine":

> "A letter of exhortation to a friend to induce him to seek. And he will reply, 'But what is the use of seeking? Nothing is seen.' Then to reply to him, 'Do not despair.' And he will answer that he would be glad to find some light, but that, according to this very religion, if he believed in it [i.e. based solely on rational proof], it will be of no use to him, and that therefore he prefers not to seek. And to answer that: 'The machine'" (*Pensées*, 247).

The tautology "the law is the law" thus loses its empty, formal character and means the following: ultimately, the law (religion, ideology) is always based on itself, on its own process of declaration and the practice of the symbolic rituals that embody it. The symbolic ritual in itself, the mere "talking about the law", is what establishes it performatively:

"Custom creates the whole of equity, for the simple reason that it is accepted. It is the mystical foundation of its authority; whoever carries it back to first principles, destroys it. Nothing is so faulty as those laws which correct faults. He who obeys them because they are just, obeys a justice which is imaginary, and not the essence of law; it is quite self-contained, it is law and nothing more. ...

The art of opposition and revolution is to unsettle established customs, sounding them even to their source, to point out their want of authority and justice. We must, it is said, get back to the natural and fundamental laws of the State, which an unjust custom has abolished. It is a game certain to result in the loss of all; nothing will be just on the balance. Yet people readily lend their ear to such arguments. They shake off the yoke as soon as they recognise it; and the great profit by their ruin, and by that of these curious investigators of accepted customs. That is why the wisest of legislators said that it was necessary to deceive men for their own good; and another, a good politician, *Cum veritatem qua liberetur ignoret, expedit quod fallatur.* ["When he asks about the truth that is to bring him freedom, it is a good thing that he should be deceived." – an inaccurate quote from Montaigne, who is half remembering St Augustine.] We must not see the fact of usurpation; law was once introduced without reason, and has become reasonable. We must make it regarded as authoritative, eternal, and conceal its origin, if we do not wish that it should soon come to an end" (*Pensées*, 294).

It is almost a pity to point out the extraordinary sub
versiveness of these Pascal's statements, which are
most impudent and "scandalous" precisely where
they seemingly aim to protect the state authority
from being undermined: the tautology "the law is
the law" means that laws have always been "lawlessly
introduced"; that their origins always hinge on
some extra-legal facticity. Therefore, we are looking
at a tautology in the Hegelian sense of the word –
a tautology that is simultaneously a pure contradiction: "the law is the law" implies precisely
the original lawlessness of the law. However, this
boundless facticity of the law – the fact that, in
the last instance, the law is justified merely with its
own declarative process and that every position
of the Legislator is always the position of a cheat,
a false pretender[3] – needs to be covered up by any
means, as this concealment is the condition for the
functioning of the law: it only functions insofar as
its subjects are deceived, insofar as they "do not feel
the truth of this unlawfulness", and to the degree
to which the authority of the law appears to them
as "justified, eternal".

This brings us back to the "depersonalised
apathy" caused by Laibach: the fundamental purpose
of Laibach's performance – the "blind" and

---

3   "No authoritative statement has any other guarantee here than its
       very enunciation, since it would be pointless for the statement to
       seek it in another signifier, which could in no way appear outside
       that locus. I formulate this by saying that there is no metalanguage
       that can be spoken, or, more aphoristically, that there is no Other
       of the Other. And when the Legislator (he who claims to lay down the
       Law) comes forward to make up for this, he does so as an impostor."
       (J. Lacan, *Écrits*, Paris, 1966, p. 813).

"mechanical" reading of totalitarian texts – is that it lets us see this internal, immanent decentralisation of ideological discourse, that it reveals the senseless "automatism", the "machine" through which ideology reproduces itself, in its naked form, so to say – i.e., precisely that it underlines the imminent "lawlessness" and tautology of the law, and therefore blocks the effectiveness of the deceit and self-concealment that is essential for the successful reproduction of ideology. What the *Nedeljski dnevnik* newspaper called the "verbal diarrhoea of the uniformed boys, read out loud" caused an "immensely nightmarish" feeling in the unsuspecting listeners: "There was nothing directly fascist in the silly answers of the uniformed boys, yet the atmosphere after the show was immensely nightmarish" (*Nedeljski dnevnik*, 3 July 1983, p. 4). By all means, this feeling can only be explained with the fact that Laibach's performance has brought to light something that is not foreign to us, but which very much concerns us in our most "genuine" intimacy: what has surfaced is that even our most well-reflected, witty, well-argued, culturally refined and noble ideological passion is ultimately based on "customs", on the automatism of the senseless ideological ritual, and that in the last instance, all our arguments and witticisms only have the role of – to summarise Pascal – presenting this ritual as "justified" and concealing its true "origin". At this point, the collocation that *Nedeljski dnevnik* offered to its readers as a swear word – "uniformed cultural workers" – turns out to be completely appropriate: the point is indeed in the "uniform", the blind symbolic ritual hidden behind the noble "cultural worker". Thus, we can finally answer the question of how Laibach, with its actions – as the group claims itself – "critically reveals the fascist aspirations in the contemporary society", even though there is no reflective, ironical-critical distance in its mimicking of the totalitarian ideological ritual (which – we should not forget this crucial fact – is by no means directly fascist, but rather represents an unidentified "totalitarianism" that contains a whole range of semi-clear allusions to Nazism, Stalinism, etc.; which, of course, makes it even more nightmarish). The misunderstanding that this may, in reality, be a sort of concealed neo-Nazism or something similar is triggered by the obvious fact that with its performance, Laibach by no means ironises the totalitarian ideological ritual: the group does nothing to establish any reflexive distance towards it, but rather keeps reiterating it completely *seriously*. Referring to our analysis of Pascal, we could say that Laibach produces a much stronger effect of alienation in relation to totalitarian ideology than any direct irony. Precisely by repeating the ideological ritual in all its "naive" literalness and self-identity: precisely by revealing the senseless ritual, it radically estranges us "in the sense" which we "experience" insofar as we are caught in ideology. The distance produced by Laibach is the distance of the very "blind" signatory mechanism towards the effect – meaning produced by this mechanism.[4]

4   Precisely the fact that in its performance, Laibach mimics a variety of contradictory and exclusive "totalitarianisms", e.g. Nazism and Stalinism, introduces an additional alienating dimension into this performance. Such a position blocks itself, because just like it is impossible to be a royalist at all without supporting a certain royal

In the subjective economy of individuals, ideology always reproduces itself through a certain distance and its subordinates/subjects never take it "literally": to face the senseless literality of the ideological ritual therefore necessarily produces a "nightmarish" feeling of alienation – an effect analogue to when a particular word, as soon as we become aware of the unusual sound of its letters, suddenly disgusts us. This distance – which, naturally, has various modes in different ideological eras – could be described based on the gap between the *(real) knowledge* and *(symbolic) belief*. We can illustrate it with a generally known psychological experience, as we call it – with something (as a rule horrible, traumatic) that "we know is so, but we still cannot believe it": the traumatic knowledge of reality has remained outside of the symbolic, the symbolic articulation keeps functioning *as if* we did not know it and we need "time to understand" in order to integrate this knowledge into our symbolic universe. The opposite version is, naturally, more common: "I know that it is not so, but I still believe it" – a form of fetishist denial ("I know that mother does not have a penis, but I still believe it [that she does]"), known to everyone especially in the form of the so-called racist "prejudice" ("I know that Jews are not to blame, but still..."). Here we should underline that such a gap between knowledge and belief, insofar as both moments are "conscious", attests to a psychotic split, a "denial of reality"; and that

dynasty – and as (Marx dixit) the only realism at all is republicanism – it is also impossible to be a "totalitarian in general" and the only "totalitarianism in general" is anti-totalitarianism.

statements of this type are – in the language of linguistic analysis – pragmatic paradoxes. Let us, for example, take a look at the statement "I know that there are no tables in the next room, but I still believe that there is a table in there": this statement is not logically contradictory – as there are no logical contradictions between the fact that there are no tables in the next room and my believing that there are tables in there. It only becomes contradictory at the pragmatic level, i.e. insofar as we take into account the position of the subject that states this sentence: without a contradiction, the subject who knows that there are no tables in the next room cannot simultaneously believe that there is a table in there. To put it differently: the subject that believes such a thing is a *split* subject. A "normal" solution to this contradiction is, of course, to *repress* the second moment, the belief, and push it into the unconscious: it is thus replaced with some substitute moment that is not in any contradiction with the first moment – this is the logic of the so-called "rationalisation". The direct split ("I know that Jews are not to blame, but still,... [I believe that they are to blame]") is replaced by a statement of the following type: "I know that Jews are not to blame, but still, it is a fact that during the development of capitalism, Jews as representatives of the financial and commercial capital were mostly usurers who benefitted from the productive labour of others"; while the direct split in the likes of "I know that God does not exist, but I still... [believe that there is a God]" is substituted with a statement like "I know that God does not exist, but I still respect religious rituals and take part in them because they consolidate ethical values and contribute to brotherhood and love among people". Such statements are a good example of what we call "lying by telling the truth": the second part of the statement – the claim that follows the collocation "but still,..." – may be completely true at the direct factual level. However, it still functions as a lie, as in the concrete symbolic economy of the context in which it appears, it functions as a confirmation of the unconscious belief that Jews are nevertheless to blame, that God nevertheless exists, etc. Without this "investment" of unconscious energy, the "internal" libidinal economy of such a statement becomes completely incomprehensible. Stalin's "diamat" is, of course, one of the pinnacles of this phenomenon. Its basic procedure when a certain pragmatic political measure that violates the theoretical principles needs to be legitimised is precisely the following: "In principle, this is true, of course; but still, the concrete circumstances...". At its core, the famous "analysis of the concrete circumstances" is nothing but a search for a rationalisation that is subsequently supposed to justify the violation of its own principles.

Based on the aforementioned gap between the (real) knowledge and (symbolic) belief, the implicit Pascalean position could thus be defined as follows: "I know that God does not exist, but I still act as if (I believed) he exists" – a self-distance, characteristic of the traditional ideology, where the part in parentheses is repressed (the belief in God that we express with our actions is unconscious). The implicit, immanent negation of this position is perhaps what is at work in the case of de Sade: already a long time ago, the most insightful analyses of his work (especially those carried out by Pierre Klossowski) have shown that de Sade's works are not merely godless: in his internal economy, he presupposes the existence of God. It is only that in this case, in comparison with Pascal, the value of the elements is reversed, i.e., the existence of God does not affirm itself at the level of belief, but rather at the level of knowledge. De Sade's protagonist acts as if he believed that God did not exist, violates all moral norms, etc., but he does all of this based on the knowledge that God does exist: this is the magic of de Sade's protagonist, the allure of his heroic-demonic position. In the case of such a protagonist, it is useless to bother proving God's existence – not because he would not be amenable to such evidence, but because deep down he knows very well that God exists, yet nevertheless rejects his existence heroically and acts in opposition to it, even though he knows this leads to eternal damnation. The position of de Sade's protagonist would therefore be "(I know that God exists, but still,) I act as if I believed God did not exist" – it is the very knowledge of God's existence that has been pushed into the subconscious.

At first glance, it seems that the same type of self-distance is all the more applicable in the case of contemporary so-called "totalitarian" ideologies, which individuals, at the subjective level, accept with a cynical "internal distance" but nevertheless take part in the "external" rituals through which these ideologies reproduce themselves. However, appearances deceive: another much more radical type of self-distance is characteristic of "totalitarian" ideologies, which has perhaps first been detected by Orwell in *1984*.

The problem with Orwell is that the vocabulary used in *1984* (Big Brother, the Thought Police, doublethink...) has long ago become a part of the everyday doxa, a self-evident definition of "totalitarianism", which has, naturally, involved a certain simplification, a realisation of a particular crucial dimension – it has to do with the idea of the "total manipulation" as implied by the established concept of "totalitarianism": the idea according to which a certain hidden subject exists that oversees the entire social process, that overlooks nothing, that "controls everything" and manages the society by judging everything. Needless to say, such a notion of the "totalitarian master" as the Big Other who has not been "deceived" already in himself, and is not himself subject to a game that he does not control, merely reproduces the immanent myth of "totalitarianism" itself... Regardless of all the shortcomings of his "1984" vision, however, at this crucial point, Orwell is far from such naivety: he is well aware that there is no such thing as manipulated gullible individuals on one side and the undeceived Manipulator who "leads the game" on the other: in "totalitarianism", the greatest believer – the only one who truly believes in the result of his manipulation – is the manipulator himself. "In our society, those who have the best knowledge of what is happening are also those who are furthest from seeing the world as it is. In general, the greater the understanding, the greater the delusion..." states 'Goldstein's book', included in *1984*. This "belief" is at the very core of the famous *double-think*: we must constantly consciously manipulate, alter the past, and cheat with the "objective reality", while simultaneously believing in the result of the manipulation with all honesty. The "totalitarian" universe is a universe of a certain psychotic split, a concealment of some completely obvious fact, rather than a universe of some "repressed secret": the indispensable knowledge that we are "deceiving" by no means affects the belief in the result of the deception. To dispel the appearance that Orwell's suppositions are merely abstract possibilities or tendencies driven to the extreme, it is enough to read, for example, Hitler's *Mein Kampf*: already the first reading reveals all the impotence of the reproaches that, in reality, Hitler merely deceives, manipulates, and counts on our "basest desires" and so on.

The problem with this sort of reproaches is not that they are not true, but in fact something much more unpleasant: they strive to kick in an open door, as what they are trying so hard to prove, Hitler completely openly admits himself: he writes at length about manipulating the "psychology of the masses", claims that the masses must be made hysterical and lied to, that problems need to be simplified, that simple and easily understandable solutions must be offered to the masses, that they need to be subjugated with a mixture of threats and promises... It is only here, however, that we come across the most dangerous trap: the erroneous conclusion that in this case, the Nazi theory therefore does not have to be taken seriously at all; that it does not deserve a severe conceptual criticism, as it does not take even itself seriously; that we have to do with a simple means of manipulation without an immanent pretension to be the truth, with an external instrument towards which its very originators exhibit a cynical distance – a trap that even such a refined critical mind as Adorno stumbled into. This is because such a perception overlooks the key fact that cannot escape an attentive reader: that regardless of his awareness of the manipulation, deep down, Hitler *completely believes in his world view* – e.g., he knows that to present Jews as enemies who hold "everything in their hands" is merely a means of manipulation, that this is only a way of channelling the aggressive energy of the masses in order to prevent its class struggle radicalisation, and so on; yet *simultaneously* he nevertheless completely unequivocally and "truly" believes that Jews are the ancient enemy. The horror of this split can be avoided as soon as we interpret it as manipulative cynicism – i.e., as soon as we see the moment of truth merely in the manipulation. This popular conception of the Nazis as ruthless cynical rulers who manipulate everything, including each other, allows us to reduce the Nazi subject to the traditional utilitarian-egoistic bourgeois subject, and thus avoid the unbearable split: the simultaneous coexistence of extreme cynicism and extreme fanaticism that, paradoxically, support each other.

Such functioning of "totalitarian" ideology could thus be defined with the term "cynical mind", which was – precisely in the sense of the specific manner of self-distance, characteristic of contemporary ideologies – introduced by Peter Sloterdijk in his work *Critique of Cynical Reason* [*Kritik der zynischen Vernunft III*, Suhrkamp, Frankfurt 1983]. However, the precondition is that we take into account the fact that the other side of cynicism always involves a certain naive belief; that – as we have just seen – cynical distance, the awareness of the manipulation, always coexists with a completely "conscious" and "naive" belief in the result of the manipulation; and that cynicism should, therefore, by no means be restricted merely to the moment of cynical distance, to disbelief. The basic logic of how the "cynical mind" operates is already indicated at the beginning of the first chapter of the aforementioned Sloterdijk's work:

"The discontent in our culture has assumed a new quality: it appears as a universal, diffuse cynicism. The traditional critique of ideology stands at a loss before this cynicism. It does not know what button to push in this cynically keen consciousness to get enlightenment going. Modern cynicism presents itself as that state of consciousness that follows after naive ideologies and their enlightenment. In it, the obvious exhaustion of ideology critique has its real ground. This critique has remained more naive than the consciousness it wanted to expose; in its well-mannered rationality, it did not keep up with the twists and turns of modern consciousness to a cunning multiple realism" (p. 33).

As it is, the traditional ideology critique always presupposes ideological consciousness, the subject of its criticism, in the form of a "naive" consciousness that is not aware of its actual presuppositions and conditions; that, in its ideological blindness, does not notice the gap between the conception of itself and what it in fact does. In the case of such a "naive" consciousness, the critical-ideological process of enlightenment can definitely follow when we make the false consciousness – as Marx puts it – "sing its own melody", thus making it reflect upon its actual presuppositions. The modern cynical consciousness, however, implies the paradox of a *reflected false consciousness:* "Cynicism is enlightened false consciousness – unhappy consciousness in modernised form" (p. 399). Cynical subjects are fully aware of the falseness of the ideological system that they adhere to, but they nevertheless keep acting that way – the reflection is included in their position in advance. Direct schizophrenia – a pathological split, a "perversely complicated structure of a consciousness that has become reflective and is almost more melancholy than false" (p. 400) – replaces the "naive" unawareness of one's own pre-suppositions. Cynical consciousness is a consciousness that by no means wishes to renounce ideological norms, but it simultaneously keeps betraying and actively denying them repeatedly in the name of a particular interest of self-preservation. If – as Marx puts it – it is characteristic of naive ideology that its subjects perceive their particular interest as the "general interest", then the cynical consciousness is completely aware of the particularity hiding behind the ideological Universality, while at the same time resigning to the necessity of the ideological mask. Marx's model of the naive ideology is the one from the first chapter of *Capital*: "They do not know it, but they are doing it" [sie wissen es nicht, aber sie tun es] – while the model of the cynical consciousness is the opposite: "They know what they are doing, but they are still doing it" [sie wissen, was sie tun, aber sie tun es]" (p. 37).

On this basis, we can also precisely demonstrate where the ordinary interpretation of Marx's model of false consciousness ("sie wissen es nicht, aber sie tun es") does not suffice – i.e., the interpretation that perceives this model in the sense of a variation of a familiar theme from *The German Ideology*, according to which, it is always necessary to strictly distinguish between what individuals imagine they are and what they in fact do, i.e. what their actual life process represents: their ideological notions are an illusory, perverted, mystified, etc., expression and the moment of their actual life process. In the context of this usual interpretation, "illusion" is thus on the side of consciousness, while the truth is on the side of being, even though this "being" (the actual life process) is, naturally, estranged already in itself and, as such, it produces a perverted consciousness. The insufficiency of such an interpretation lies in the fact that the moment of deception – the "illusion" that is at work already in the middle of "being" itself, in the centre of what individuals "do" – is lost on it. Let us, for example, take a look at money fetishism: consciously, the individuals who are subject to commercial and monetary circumstances know, of course, that "money is not God", that it is merely a material manifestation of social relations; nevertheless, in the actual process of exchange, they act *as if* money were, in its direct sensual materiality, an embodiment of general value. What such individuals "do not know" is thus an "illusion", a fetishist perversion that they adhere to in their actual life process: in light of Marx's famous sentences in the first chapter of *Capital* – that if we say that the Roman law and the German law are two kinds of law, this is completely self-evident; yet if we say that the abstraction of law manifests itself in the form of the Roman and Greek law, the relationship becomes mystical – that in light of these sentences we should never forget even for a moment that in their everyday consumerism, citizens by no means believe that the Law in general manifests itself as distinct forms of law. Their everyday ideology is nominalist through and through: they believe that the Roman and the German law are two kinds of law. The problem, however, is that in their process of exchange, they *act* as if the abstraction of Law manifests itself in the distinct forms of law, and that they do not know *that*!

Only on this basis can we comprehend the internal tension and paradox of the "they know what they are doing, but they are still doing it" model of the cynical mind: if the "they do not know it, but they are doing it" model of false consciousness were comprehended as a simple split between the false consciousness and reality, the model of cynical consciousness could only mean the simple alignment of consciousness and being, an undivided, "true" consciousness of individuals who are conscious of their being, who know what they are doing. However, the true dimension of the cynical consciousness reveals itself only when we stem from the already developed fact that the "illusion" is at work at the centre of being itself, and that it defines the very actions of individuals in contradiction with their consciousness – in this case, the model of the cynical mind means "they know that with their actions, they act as if they believed (in the fetishist illusion), but they still act as if they believed."

Sloterdijk develops the basic logic of cynical consciousness through the triad *naive ideology – kynicism – cynicism*, which must undoubtedly be interpreted as a cynical repetition/mimicking of the Hegelian triad: first, we have a certain naive, elevated ideological system that "takes itself seriously"; a system full of "noble" moral guidelines, etc. The first reaction to this system – a direct "negation" – would be kynicism, for example that of Diogenes: the fundamental experience of kynicism is the experience of the gap between the false superiority of the "official" ideology and the actual reality of the banal, everyday life; the experience of how silly and frail the superiority of the official ideology is; and at the same time the experience that particular dirty interests, violence, and ruthless authority are always hiding behind the elevated nobility of the official ideology. Ever since Diogenes, the means of a kynical reaction to the official ideology has more often involved parody – rebuttal by confronting concrete real-life examples that reveal the true function of the official ideology – rather than rational argumentation. Let us take this extremely simplified model: a kynical reaction to an elevated speech of an official politician about the nobility of sacrificing oneself for one's homeland is not to rebut the sense of such sacrifice with arguments, but to confront such statements with their entire context, i.e. – to put it in terms of linguistic analysis – to criticise pragmatically rather than logically: the answer would be "they preach sacrifice because they know that is the only way to retain power", or something similar. Ever since the beginning, such kynical reactions have been the key moment of Marx's critical-ideological process: let us merely underline the recurrent sarcasm in *The German Ideology* and analyses of the 1848 revolution. At this point, we could, at the stylistic level, refer to Bakhtin's distinction between the "carnivalesque" tradition of dialogue, parody, etc., in opposition to the "official" tradition of monologic seriousness. Therefore, the kynical reaction, in its provocative form, reveals the gap between the elevated ideological seriousness and the reality that calls this seriousness a lie and ridicules it. However, the answer to this kynical provocation, that is much more effective than direct repression in upholding the naive ideological system, is a violent return to "seriousness", or any direct denial of the gap: cynicism.

"We reserved the concept of cynicism for the reply of the rulers and the ruling culture to the kynical provocation. They definitely see that there is an element of truth in it, but proceed with oppression. From now on, they know what they do" (p. 400).

Thus, cynicism would be that point of the perverted "synthesis" where the dominant culture itself implicitly completely admits to the particular interests of the domination concealed behind its universal ideological postulates, yet keeps preserving this universal mask in the interest of self-preservation. One example is the point where capitalists determine that they do not need to steal from the workers directly with any harsh means, as the very framework of the "just" market exchange in itself ensures exploitation. To put it differently: a particular ideological field always articulates the "everyday" experience through the categories of good vs. evil, legal vs. illegal, fair vs. unfair. Thus, for example, the ordinary bourgeois everyday life hinges on the opposition between the legal enrichment through reselling, banking, investing, etc., and the illegal violent robbery and fraud. At this point, cynicism would be that point of perversion that Brecht so very wittily pointed out with the famous sarcasm in *The Threepenny Opera*: "What is the robbing of a bank compared to the founding of a bank!" – the point where we experience how "legal" enrichment is, in comparison with the direct crime of robbery, in fact a much worse and far more successful form of theft, as it is also legal and wrapped in an aura of fairness... The old pervert who, with an experienced smile, preaches how crucial morality is – or the government crook who, with righteous indignation, persecutes small-time "illegal" hustlers etc. in order to protect an institutionalised fraud – represent superb cynical characters. Roughly put, the greatest cynical wisdom is that honesty is the most successful form of deception, morality the highest form of debauchery, and truth the superb form of lying. The old wisdom that lies are short-lived is opposed by Oscar Wilde's famous cynicism, which – by the way – is thoroughly confirmed by the real socialist practices in the field of journalism: "If one tells the truth, one is sure, sooner or later, to be found out". With precisely this logic of cynicism we should – as Sloterdijk underlines – comprehend the fact that in the early bourgeois tradition, protagonists (from Dr Faustus to Don Juan) who "made a deal with the devil" and openly, in principle, lived "beyond good and evil" would, in the end, be punished a hundred times worse than they deserved in accordance with their actions: according to the folk tradition, Dr Faustus was torn apart by bestial spirits so that his brain and blood flew everywhere and stuck to the walls; while Don Juan was swallowed by hellfire. The rage aimed against them does not have as much to do with their actions – their "crimes" are hilarious in comparison with those of the vast majority of politicians – as with their attitude: the fact that they in principle set themselves apart "beyond good and evil", that they turned their existential position into an *ethical stance* in the strictest sense: they made decisions that they followed "beyond the principle of comfort", regardless of pleasure, benefits, aspirations, etc. The demand for their terrible punishment to make an example out of them expresses cynicism par excellence:

> "This address is cynical in the most modern sense because it contains a sardonic [hämisch] restoration of morality by the one about whom we know anyway that he offends against it in principle" (Sloterdijk, op. cit., p. 665).

This cynicism – whose good example would be the final scene of Mozart's *Don Giovanni*, the "moral" at the end of the story (after the death of Don Giovanni) – affects Don Juan but not Casanova, as the difference between them is precisely in the fact that Casanova does not elevate his activities to an ethical level and therefore does not threaten anything or anyone: he has no problem taking part in the dominant cynical comedy.

Based on this definition of the cynical-obscene functioning of ideology, we can, in conclusion, return to the claim that Laibach's performance needs to be understood as the staging of Hegel's dialectics of tautology, which is simultaneously a pure contradiction, and argue in favour of this claim somewhat more broadly. Wherein lies the Hegelian subversion of tautology? Let us take the statement "God is God": according to its form, this statement is a judgement, i.e. its first part ("God is ...") conveys an impression that the second part would give a particular predicate, a definition of the fundamental empty generality (e.g. God is the wisest, omnipotent, etc.); but in this case, the second part ("… God") disappoints, as it merely repeats what has already been said. Therefore, the statement "God is God" is a contradiction. The first God ("God is …") is a positive generality which encompasses all its predicates; while its neutral medium, the second God ("… God) is a negative generality that negates all of its particular contents. Let us remember Lacan's interpretation of Racine's *Athalie*: the first God is good, calming, the God of bliss in the afterlife; while the second God is the God of God's wrath – the God that incites fear, a terrible God, more horrific than all the horrors of this world. At this point, we could also refer to Marx's frequently mentioned paradox from *The Class Struggles in France*, where republicanism appears as that paradoxical type of royalism that embodies the very origin of royalism: the statement "God is God" must be interpreted in the same manner as "royalism is republicanism": generality meets itself in a negative form in its own ranks.

The same goes for Laibach's performance: Laibach appears as an obscene subversion of the totalitarian ritual; i.e., the very form of its performance states and defines that we are dealing with subversion. However, in terms of "content", our expectations are not met: we are disappointed because we get the same – a repetition of the totalitarian ritual – instead of a critical distance, ridicule, and so on. The "message" is thus clear enough: obscene parody, transgressions, etc., of the ideological ritual of the authorities are in vain – not because this ritual is invulnerable or indestructible, but, quite the opposite, because this very ritual in itself represents the highest form of obscenity. At this point, we can paraphrase Brecht's thought from *The Threepenny Opera*, stated above: What is a measly avant-garde "provocation", against the provocation employed by the authorities! How much more cynical is a single political declaration than all the "radical" subcultural performances put together! How much more ridicule and distance towards "ethical earnestness and dedication" is contained in ordinary reasoning behind a bureaucratic decision than in avant-garde derision and mockery of the "official" speech's "seriousness"! The Great Punker – the cynical "outlaw" that will not be "caught in the game" – are the *Authorities Themselves*.

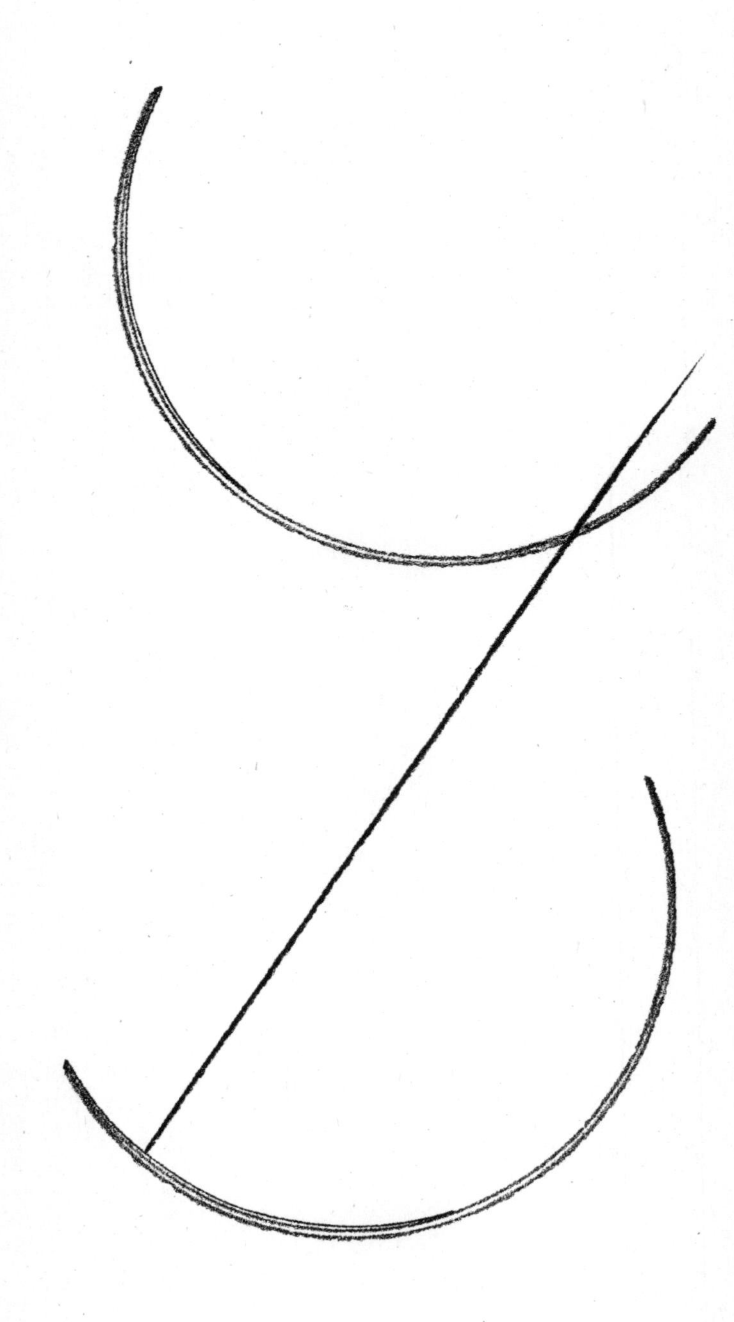

ALONG CAME TURK...
Zoja Skušek

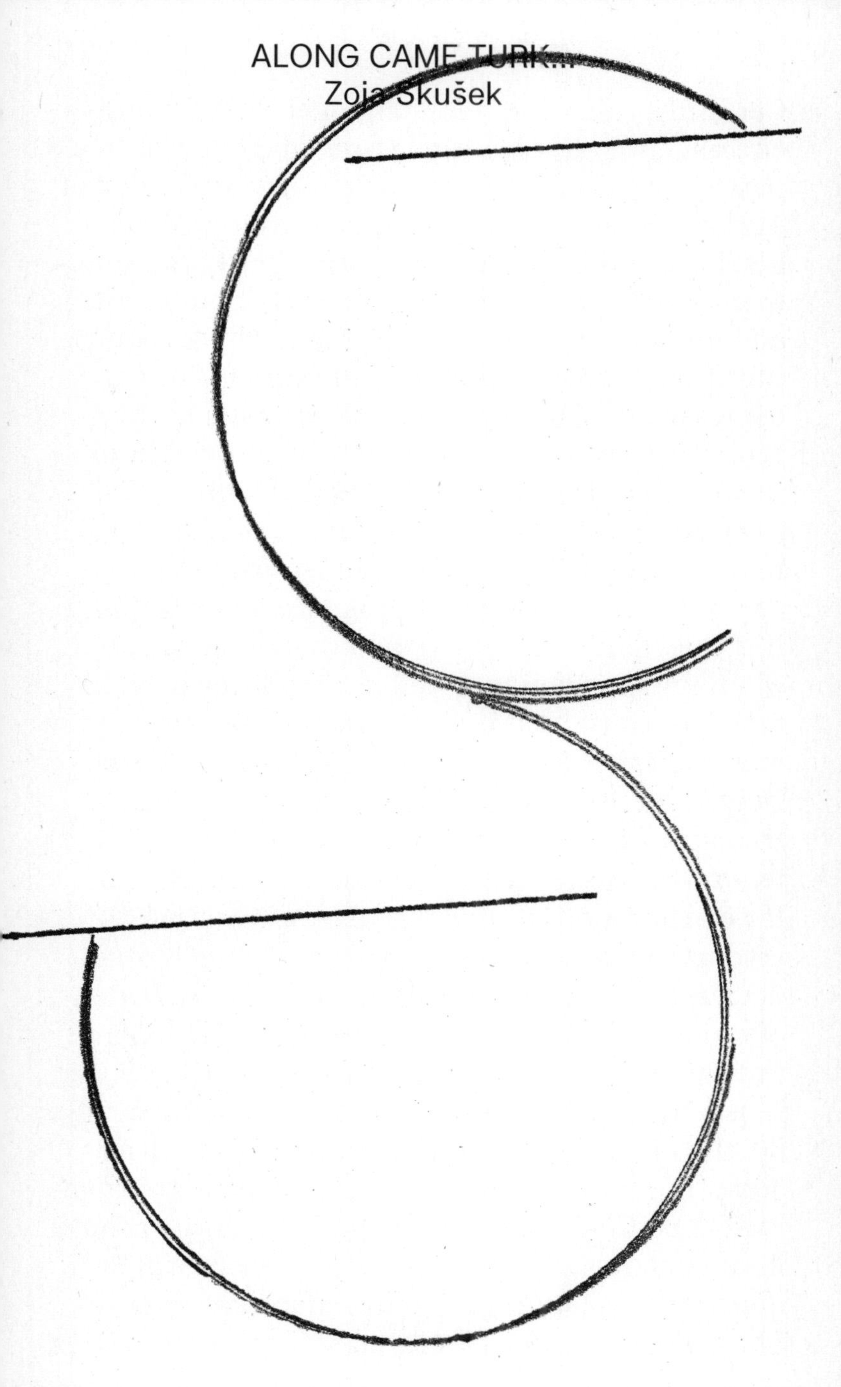

Certainly, this statement can mean that a Turkish citizen, coming back from a foreign country to his native village somewhere in the Anatolian plains of Turkey, came to Ljubljana while travelling down her/his route. In this case, the meaning of the statement would seemingly overlap with its referent, and it *precisely* represents *the reason* why it is quite improbable that we would come across such an expression in a newspaper report about a traffic accident on the road to Zagreb. The participant in the accident is just a person, an individual of a certain age, married or not, but *in addition* to that undoubtedly a Turk, and a semi-German, i.e. a member of a segregated proletarian population. It is this nuance in explanation that determines whether the meaning would be glued-down to the referent, thus making the sentence, so to say, *meaningless*: it either says too much or too little. Despite all the information on this hypothetical transitory passenger's état civil (civil status), his nationality is as much evident as it is coincidental. If we in addition say that the person is a "Turk", it is somehow redundant. Precisely for being redundant and saying too little, it opens up the question of what could be the cause for such an addition in the reportage. The apparent absence of such a cause is usually inhabited by the "most probable" meaning, i.e. the ideological one. The information warns about the transmitter of the news since in the ideological context constituted by the absence of cause it must necessarily lead to an anthropomorphic question: "What did the journalist want to say?" Thus, when a reader already presumes the subject of a stereotypical journalistic product, s/he displays, while hiding it from her/himself, that s/he has been *already* interpellated by that "information" into a subject of ideological discourse. In reality, the reader speaks through her/his journalist as a subject, but only as much as the ideological discourse as such speaks through her/him, meaning that it is a discourse without a subject or, more accurately, a discourse that constitutes its own subject(s). Then the information, due to this "absence of cause" in the report reads: "Sleep-deprived Turks – danger on our roads".

However, it is interesting that not only that sentence but any other of that kind will not produce an interpellation effect: "The exploitation of the workforce during labor time equals the destruction of its bearer during free time". We would never ascribe this kind or similar types of thoughts to a journalist – because the discourse within which such a thought can be produced needs no foundations in some presumed subject with hidden chauvinist prejudices. As far as the materialist analysis of the question of free time demands the minimum of scientific discourse, I cannot delegate my own impure thoughts to some presumed subject since scientific discourse is in no way interpellating me into a subject position as an individual with specific (i.e. abstractly general) psycho-physical complexes. Thus, a reader can presuppose the subject of the "report" only if discourse has already established that subject. This means that if a discourse is specifically constructed as an (ideological) message that appeals to its receiver, which is always an individual,

it always catches her/him in its meshes and interpellates her/him into a subject.

This is a secular example of the functioning
of ideology done in the same manner as Althusser
used Biblical examples. However, we have by
doing this only taken into account the ideological
mechanism. Now we must ask ourselves what is
the material basis of that discursive mechanism.
Althusser was very cautious about it: he only
claimed that ideology has a material existence,
as in, for example, in the discursive functioning
of, ideological (state) apparatuses. Therefore,
he opened two possible routes for research: one
concerned with material discursive mechanisms
that produce the ideological effect and the other
that concerns the (state) ideological apparatuses.
The first problem field was taken on by Michel
Pêcheux, while the second was researched by Pierre
Macherey and Étienne Balibar who discovered
that the school apparatus is the basis of a special
ideological discourse – the one of national literature. However, their thesis was in fact dismissed:
namely, they anticipated the answer to the question
of specific relation of determination between (ideological) discursive mechanisms and (state) ideological
apparatuses. Certainly, those two kinds of research do
not contradict one another, and at the first glance we
could unite them in some kind of a stratified determination: an ideological effect (for example, an aesthetic
effect) is determined by discursive mechanisms (of
national literature) whose "material base" is given by
the ideological (state) apparatuses (capitalist general
and compulsory school education).

The danger of establishing such a determinative chain consists, of course, in that we can automatically (mechanically) extend it and claim the following: the material basis of the ideological apparatuses of the bourgeois state is the capitalist economy. The capitalist school was certainly established "with an intention" to train the workforce in its specific abstract and free form that is needed by the capitalist labour process. It is *precisely* because of that it has no intention of using national literature as "its own" specific ideology. Yet, the school as the factory of the workforce (thus: as an apparatus for the reproduction of the relations of production) *cannot do without* its special ideology – national literature and its product – national language (as "mother tongue"). Even the most utilitarian and entirely pragmatically oriented schooling system cannot execute its banal tasks without a poetic supplement – as it can be seen clearly in, for example, the most recent school reform in Slovenia. Literature has its own foundation in the school apparatus, but it "serves" another social purpose. If it serves in the production of the workforce, it must, in the first place, produce its "own" ideology. It cannot reproduce the relations of production unless it bases itself on the ideology of the "mother tongue" that is created by literary discourse. National literature has its foundation in the school apparatus that is itself based on the national literature: the foundation of ideology is based on ideology.

This pattern is somewhat too extensive, and ideology in this sense means it includes, without any distinctions, an ideological effect, the mechanism that produces that effect and discourse within which that mechanism operates. Thus, we must say in a more concrete way: the foundation of discourse is discourse. Consequently, an analysis that remains "within" the discursive horizon can lead to results that are pertinent for historical materialism. All of this is, of course, valid under the condition that we don't obscure the "foundational" pattern that we have just established. It is stating that discourse is not equivalent to itself, and that it is the space opened up by that unevenness that allows us to populate it with an "ideological apparatus". (We can inhabit it with some other institution, given the type of mechanism operating within the discourse, but we are here concerned with a specific example.) Above all, this means that the "material existence" of ideology is not something "external" to discourse, and that the material conditions of discourse are always already discursive. It cannot be otherwise, as soon as we acknowledge that "communicational pattern" with its constituent parts represents an ideological effect or, more accurately, the effect of a distinctive historical ideological functioning of discourse.

The functioning of that structural determination or over-determination – as Althusser would put it by borrowing the notion from Freud – can be discerned already in the most trivial of all the wisdom of historical materialism. It roughly states that the material basis and the determinant of national language is the capitalist economy since it *demands* or *needs* for its very survival a continuous and homogenous national space guaranteed by the state. This thesis, despite being somewhat approximate and general, is basically accurate since the determinant as the condition of its possibility presupposes something that is determined by that very determinant. We could even say that the state as the tool of class exploitation, i.e. as an "institution", is possible because of a short circuit that places among the conditions of possibility precisely what is being determined. In that way, the reproduction of the relations of production, which is secured by the state and its apparatuses, is, at the same time, the preproduction of classes or, as Althusser puts it, it is the class struggle that constitutes the classes.

Only in this precise meaning is it possible to claim that an "immanent" analysis of discourse provides results pertinent to historical materialism: structural determination is a determination that operates through the short circuit of the structure, and that short circuit is a "discursive mechanism". If discourse is the very condition of possibility of discourse, we can easily capture in it the structural determination in its "pure" form.

This constitutes the reason why we can take into account the aforementioned example as a completely literary statement – for instance as a line from a description of a historical event. Then it could mean that Hasan Pasha, with his 25000 soldiers, arrived at Sisak [referring to the battle between Ottoman Empire and combined Christian forces in 1593 in Sisak, Croatia]. We can sense that such a sentence could be more appropriate for that context, as we can say that the "Turk" is besieging Sisak. However, the "meaning" of the expression in that appropriate context appears somehow suspended in the void if we compare it with its referent: in any case, the difference of 24999 people is too large to be ignored. Unless, of course, we would think of that Turk precisely as Hasan Pasha, as we could say: "Hasan Pasha is besieging Sisak". But, then we must ask ourselves how the word "Turk" has meaning only if behind the person it signifies stand 25000 Turks, preferably armed to their teeth. The upshot of such an assumption is still contained in that it offers us a solution in military organisation for a semantic problem: according to the fiction of military regulations, the general is also a soldier.

If we say: "We can signify with the word 'Turk' only someone with 25000 Turks behind him" then we can surely immediately ask ourselves how can we use the word "Turk" already for the first among those 25000. It would be possible if the Turkish army would make a circle in which the soldiers would sit on each other's knees – each one would sit on everybody else and, at the same time, support everyone else. In the same vein, it could be said that every soldier carries a general's baton in his bag – while the only inconvenience would be that only one of them is carrying it in his arms.

It is in the space between 25000 Turkish soldiers and the "Turk" that we should look for the *meaning* of the statement that we took as our example. It doesn't depict in any way the events at the battlefield near the river Kupa (near Sisak), but it *operates* within social relations about which it remains *silent*. "Turk", as the personification of evil, i.e. of both figuratively and literally something non-Christian, represents a trigger that is supposed to subjectivise the reader-listener of that "objective" information about the Turkish advances. It is a pathway that is supposed to subjectivise her/him in accordance with the dictates of the society that thinks and constitutes itself as the *antemurale christianitatis*, the defensive wall of Christianity. The paradox of personification contained in the statement is needed as to, after the statement was articulated, constitute a belief that upholds a class feudal society, which places its internal conflicts at the doorstep of the Sublime Porte (the Sultan's government in Istanbul).

According to this, the expression is just a theorem derived from the ideological axiom that allows the reproduction-constitution of class repression and, in short, serves to impose the ideological demand that we add to each one of the Christians one Turk that assaults them. That demand, by establishing a spectre of a Turk, is constitutive of the Christian community itself and, of course, particularly necessary since the Ottoman Empire has ceased to exist.

The logic of that "sylleptic" noun consists not only in that it produces the effect as if among all the Turks there is, in addition, a "Turk in general". Its special pragmatic value consists in that we can, in encountering each and every element of the Turkish multitude, act like we are dealing with that "Turk in general". A sylleptic noun can be introduced at any point within the space that it determines – we can recognise in every Turk the "Turk in general" or, more accurately, we can substitute every Turk with the

"Turk". That last pattern is especially rewarding since it simultaneously means: 1. with that simple operation that adds *yet another* element, i.e. the name of that multitude, the elements of that multitude become mutually interchangeable; 2. with that operation by which we *recognise* in one element the name of the multitude that it belongs to, we *deceive* ourselves, we become confused in the same way as we "substitute" in our daily lives a stranger with a familiar person on the street. That self-deception is, of course, constitutive of any kind of racism. It also explains why the analyses that perceive ideology only as a deception fall short of a real explanation: ideology is a deception, only if it is primarily a self-deception, and it serves some particular purpose. This is an operation, constitutive of an ideological community, that each of the individuals must perform "on her/himself" if s/he belongs to that community at all.

The logical pattern of that operation is, of course, too general: not every "syllepsis" is a necessary support for an ideological discourse. For example, the existence of "horse" is necessary in the biological scientific discourse: in zoology, *genus* has a real existence. Without commodities and money in general there is no commodity exchange, and the notional existence of money in the political economy prevents us from thinking about the problem of value: in the same manner, the "Turk" prevents us from thinking about the class struggle within the borders of Christendom. Turk is the trigger that will transform an entrepreneur, tradesman, peasant, nobleman, or soldier into a "Christian" under one God equal for all Christians. The fact that God has to wear a distorted mask of the archetypical Asian is as much a matter of his teleological non-figurativeness as it is a suspicious example of how ideology must contradict itself if it wants to give birth to an institution: God must ride around on a small Bosnian horse if he wants to keep his sheep at bay.[1]

Acts of this kind, which are supported by the church as the number one (state) apparatus and which operate in a different manner on the ideological body of the ruler, certainly seem wholeheartedly naïve in comparison to the contemporary bourgeois state that developed the ideological dominant of its activity through the "pluralism of ideas". Althusser's pattern for the analysis of state with its simplistic schematics – (repressive) state apparatus *plus* ideological apparatuses – has offered new conceptual tools for the analysis of contemporary class domination, and thus opened the horizon for successive analyses among which those that Poulantzas have made are the most important.[2] The analysis of the bourgeois state's ideological "pluralism" can be of crucial help in researching the contemporary function of (class) "power". Lately, alongside the traditional Marxist stance, which is somewhat static since it presupposes some intermediate, more or less

1   It is enough to take a look at the decrees of the Holy Roman Emperor Maximilian I towards the population of Kranj to be able to see that Turkish infidelity was always an argument in favour of taxation.

2   Nicos Poulantzas, *State, Power, Socialism*, Verso, London, 1980.

"concealed" power, the theory of "micro" power has gained currency above all. It is developed primarily by Deleuze and Foucault, and its main weakness is that it overextends the question of power since, according to that theory, we can encounter some kind of power at each and every step (the "power" of power). At the same time, this analysis enables us to pose more accurately the questions of (national) literature, and its (ideological) aesthetic effect, which Macherey and Balibar assertively placed within the number one ideological apparatus of the bourgeois state – the school.

The state, as the tool of class repression, primarily reproduces certain historical class relations, meaning that it provides a specific substratum upon which class struggle can commence at all. That "substratum" of class struggle is certainly not neutral since it represents by itself one of the *stances* in the class struggle. The state is thus one of the "parties" in the class struggle, but it is a party that determines the space and the scope in which the parties involved in class struggle clash with each other. This means that the *state itself* is a party in its struggle against the repressed classes. This double function, as the organiser of the space of class struggle and as a party in that struggle, enables the state to act in two ways: through (repressive) state apparatus and through ideological (state) apparatuses. This scheme of Althusser could be translated into a more traditional speech: state operates in the field of the judicial-political superstructure, "in itself", i.e. in the realm of the state, and also in the field of civil society, i.e. in its opposite.

Although the division on repressive and ideological apparatuses is certainly not identical to the division on (political) state and civil society, we can nevertheless say that the ideological apparatuses are anchored predominantly in civil society. It is the ideological discourse that speaks to individuals that comprise civil society, and it is what establishes them as (distinct) subjects: as much as ideological apparatuses are not operating entirely within civil society, they are still necessarily producing it.

Ideological apparatuses, of course, also reach into the field of the legal-political superstructure since it is in the bourgeois "autonomous" state that the organisation of power is predominantly ideological. It is that political-state sphere, the sphere of state power, which is the institution that *invests in a class manner* non-class and pre-class relations of domination, which have been pushed back into civil society (family relations, domination in terms of age or sex, various forms of meritocracy and mandarinism of experts, etc.). That sphere of state power is the tool with which the relations of class domination are being divided into "non-class" relations of power within civil society. With that class distribution "local" relations of domination and subordination become pertinent in terms of class.

That is why it is the sphere of state-political power in the narrow sense that represents the instance through which the civil society is constituted in its class and state-making pertinence. Hence, only by the means of state political power, the opposite between the "state" and the "civil society" is being constituted. The investment in and the occupation of "civil society" with its class pertinence is happening precisely through establishing the opposition between the political state and the civil society. That opposition is what ultimately constitutes civil society in its sole class pertinence.

Therefore, if the state intervenes, in terms of class, in civil society (i.e. it "constitutes-supports it") so as to "occupy", in terms of class, various heterogeneous local power structures, it becomes clear that the discourse, with which that class investment is affirmed, cannot be uniform and unified. To put it in more simplistic terms, the state must speak to families and heads of families in a different way than to the mandarins in academia. Certainly, that is the reason why the state "occupies" non-class and pre-class family structures by means of a purposefully organised state apparatus – the family, while the "academic" field, inherited from previous (social) formations, of the bourgeois state incorporates with the help of the ideological apparatus number one – the school.

On the other hand, the state must still unify the field of its differential interventions in order to ensure that all those regional interventions serve one and the same purpose. Accordingly, ideological apparatuses are unified under the domination of one of the apparatuses, and that "institutional" dominant is undoubtedly guaranteed by the dominant of ruling ideology – the ideology of ruling class. However – as Poulantzas correctly emphasises – the capitalist state has one more important homogenizing task to fulfill: it must uniformly *atomise* the field of its activity, divide it into individual subjects, the homogenous atoms of the social field.

Consequently, state intervention in class terms must act in two contradictory ways: on the one hand, it must *heterogenise* its class discourse of political rule and adapt it to its own different "headlines"or, better yet, goals, while on the other, it must *homogenise* that very field of its activity by transforming it into civil society comprised of "isolated individuals". It is this homogenizing atomization-individuation of headlines-goals that represents the investment of that field that is pertinent in terms of class rule (domination). If a class state would capture individuals in its meshes only in a manner of adding to various pre-existing structures of power its own discourse of class domination, then its domination would still be purely external. Local structures of power would be included in the class relations only from the outside, but that still wouldn't represent a true class investment – i.e. those structures wouldn't yet be immediately pertinent in terms of class. However, if those structures are firstly divided from the inside into persons, individuals as subjects, by the (bourgeois) class discourse, and then "recomposed" again, it means that those somewhat "archaic" structures cannot exist at all without the class mediation. It is this that makes them truly "internally" class relevant, and they become by the fact of their mere existence something that supports-reproduces the relations of class domination.

Therefore, in order for the (bourgeois) state to be able to invest in class terms the field of its (ideological, discursive) activity, the field of its (ideological) discourse, its own discourse must be *heterogeneous*. However, if that investment should be a class one, then it must secure *homogenization* within the (bourgeois) state.

This contradictory double task is more easily achievable than it at first seems: primarily, its solution certainly doesn't consist in abolishing contradictions – the contradiction of state's mandate is resolved in a way that it is, namely, being reproduced and preserved. Thus, the difficulty lies not in the fact that contradiction couldn't be resolved, it is the other way around: the danger lies in the possibility that it could be really abolished.

If the state intervention must be simultaneously discursive and class based, then it is, of course, necessarily ideological. But, if it is purely ideological, it can only be individualizing, individualizing in a manner of subjectivation, i.e. it can only perform atomizing functions. Thus, the homogeneity of ideological discourse is already guaranteed by the fact that discourse is ideological.

(All this is on the provision that we are thinking of the classic "autonomous" bourgeois state. In other socio-economic formations, where the so-called "extra-economic coercion" is needed, ideology cannot, of course, act in a "pure" manner. Ideology is thus much more unified since it is not "pure", meaning that it is less internally differentiated [it needs less ideological apparatuses] and it is connected with economic and repressive relations.)

When the ideological discourses (of the state) become ideological, and they always do, they can also become irreducibly "different" and heterogeneous.

But, if those discourses "can be" heterogeneous, then what unifies them? What unifies discourses that are both ideological and different from each other?

It is the virtue of being both ideological and different that unifies discourses that are ideological and different from each other.

Therefore, they are brought together or *unified* by an ideological matrix that belongs to "all" the different discourses. So, what makes "all" those different discourses ready to spontaneously, and thus ideologically, acknowledge it as their common, unified matrix? "All" those different discourses are quite surely ready to acknowledge that they are expressing themselves in the same language, meaning, of course, common "people's" or, "mother" language.

It is the *national language* as the mother tongue that represents the ideological matrix of all different (ideological) discourses in a bourgeois democratic state.

Starting from this assertion about the ideological activity of class domination, we can derive the following conclusion: class state-political power in the capitalist social formation "is" the irreducibility of differences between all (autonomous, ideological, i.e. "all" since they "all" facilitate the ideological occupation) discourses in the bosom of the national language.

This "bosom" of the mother tongue is certainly mythological, but that doesn't make it less efficient: when we say that it is "mythological", by that we mean that it is always constituted retroactively, and thus "nothing" can escape it. ("All" discourses fall into it, since it instantly absorbs every difference with which a "new" discourse would claim its separateness:

the mother tongue represents a differential matrix of traits that make up the differences, the differentiation of differences, and, above all, the differences between discourses.) Thus this retroactively constituted *structural* foundation is ideologically comprehended as the pre-existing *source*.

In this way, the mother language represents the mythological matrix of an all-encompassing *translatability* of different ideological discourses. If those discourses are ideological, they are, in accordance with that, translatable into the mother language, which only means that they are translatable into each other: the mother language is really *nothing other* than precisely that translatability. Mother language is *not "yet another"* discourse in addition to them all – it is their common feature. Nevertheless, we can say this in other terms, and thus even better explain the mythological status of national language: mother language is precisely that "yet another" discourse into which any discourse is translatable into, on the provision that it is ideological and state-constitutive while the possibility of translation is *not yet* realised. It can be realised only with some other equally "partial" ideological discourse – meaning that every (ideological) discourse can *represent* the mother language for some other (ideological) discourse. (Thus we have the insertion of "power" between each and every discourse.)

It is this translatability into (if it is possible) the established ideological discourses which is the measure of statehood and state-constitutiveness of every discourse. And the other way around: as much as a discourse is translatable, it is that much ideological.

That is the reason why, within bourgeois culture, a special place is reserved for "critique" as the practice of ideological translation of "artefacts" into the discourse of dominant ideology. That practice of translation is, of course, at the same time the practice of disregarding the untranslatable elements. The "critique" (in the meaning that was introduced by Igor Vidmar and that is dominant in Slovene culture) is thus a practice of class struggle as ideological struggle from the vantage point of dominant ideology. From the vantage point of non-dominant ideologies, the critique, so to speak, is impossible: it is too much "creative" to be regarded as critique at all.

It is clear that the demand for translatability will run into huge, properly speaking insurmountable difficulties at least in two cases when languages are not constitutively tied to the maternal national language: in the case of theoretical language and in the case of "artistic" expression. Of course, the bourgeois state seeks to occupy both of those fields with its ideological apparatus number one, i.e. with the school apparatus, the educational one (mother language) – the educational system (based on theoretically constituted technique). That example vividly shows how this class occupation happens when the state encroaches upon languages which, of course, exist "before" it, alongside it and, especially, without it.

The most important for the class ideological occupation of literature is, of course, the dominant

ideological effect, while in the field of artists' language – the aesthetic effect. If we approach this issue
in such terms, then all previous quarrels about the
opposition between aesthetic autonomy and the
political-popular service are immediately dropped.
Moreover, it makes visible the crucial role of those
disputes in the class-power occupation of the field
of "artistic" language. The discourse that produces
the ideological aesthetic effect is as much people-
constitutive and state-constitutive as it is autonomous: its autonomy is the condition for the production of its effect, and the aesthetic effect is
a specific effect of class occupation in the field of
"artistic" discourse. If the "artistic" discourse
wouldn't be autonomous, it wouldn't be heterogeneous vis-à-vis other discourses – thus, it wouldn't
be translatable, meaning that it wouldn't unfold
in the mother language. And the other way around:
if it should be state-constitutive, it must be able
to be expressed in the mother language, and thus
translatable, therefore "different from other discourses", "autonomous"...

The people-constitutive and state-constitutive
functions of literature represent thus its aesthetic
mandate as well as its people-serving programme,
an aesthetic programme, with which Levstik[3] has
command over literature in order for it to become
such that

---

3   Fran Levstik (1831 – 1887) was a Slovene writer, political activist, playwright, and critic. He was one of the most prominent exponents of the
Young Slovene political movement that fought for Slovenian national
self-determination with its own particular language and culture.

...a Slovene would be able to recognise a Slovene in the book, the same as he sees his own reflection in the mirror.

It is therefore pointless to complain that within a nation, that wasn't established by the bourgeois state but which instead had to do that "by itself", "out of" the literature (i.e. "from" the bourgeois class investment in the field of language), its literature or art in general is in any way "blocked" from realising its mandate of overseeing people. The supposed "suppression" and "deracination" are merely snowflakes at the battleground of ideological struggle as they represent a non-antagonistic opposition within one and the same (bourgeois) ideological horizon. The difference lies somewhere else: a bourgeois state that encounters an already established "artistic" production in the field of language must intervene in such fields in a very differentiated and subtle manner, and construct a series of ideological apparatuses, etc. Nevertheless, it never fully succeeds to completely enclose the field of the so-called traditional culture, thus making the class nature of ideological investment completely obvious. The state, within such a type of development that Slovenes are familiar with, much more naturally grew out of the aesthetic effect, thus making the class-ideological occupation even more mystified. The aesthetic effect retroactively structures, in a teleological manner, the entire field of language in such a way that the state ideological apparatuses in that field can be much simpler. The school apparatus can be much more rudimentary –

but it can also completely lose all connections with the field of language. (In this way, for example, with the most recent Slovene school reform the state through its own ideological apparatus is precisely being "severed" [separated] from the field of language.) This means that debates about "blockage" and "deracination" are precisely as old as Slovene artistic expression, and this is necessary due to the fact that artistic production had always been radically slipping away from the class ideological occupation. Such a "debate" that artificially separates something that is one and the same precisely represents the mode of bourgeois class intervention. It comprises of occupation of the field of language at the moment when that field fairly successfully escaped such an occupation, but still, such an ideological concern can only reproduce the myth of wild-grown quasi-natural development from language to people, and from people to the state, a myth that represents a specific form of mystification of the class struggle.

The most important advance of bourgeois ideology consists, of course, in replacing the folk-loric Turk with a narcissistic Slovene. Although feudal Christian society is explicitly internally structured (the obvious social "inequalities" and the "extra-economic coercion"), it must be mediated by an "external" ideological figure. In that way, bourgeois society can still mediate itself on its own on a provision that it is "ideologically" atomised, "levelled-out", homogenised. More accurately: it is this "internal" mediation that levels it out and homogenises it.

Levstik's programmatic saying could support the traditional (bourgeois) explanation to be wrestled out of the materialist clinch with a remark that the above mentioned epochal sentence may be truly an aesthetical judgement in its form, but that it is, in terms of its contents, certainly people-constitutive. That could be correct up to a certain point. It would be accurate precisely up to that edge beyond which such an explanation is not visible: the edge of the mother language. This already proves that it speaks *within* the horizon described precisely by that sentence: such an interpretation is thus only executing that programme, although it thinks – precisely because it is self-confident – that it is "interpreting, commenting [on]" it. In this case, a special procedure is required to elevate Levstik to a position of meta-language, but precisely in doing that the commentary becomes his discourse-object whose meta-language inevitably becomes Levstik's national-bourgeois programme.

Nevertheless, let's for a moment, take this explanation as it is: let's say, for example, that only the form is aesthetical. Truth be told, there is something "aesthetical" in the sentence: in its banal meaning it "distances from" only from its everyday usage but also from the norm. In a normal sentence in the place of the other "Slovene" would be a personal reflexive pronoun: "a Slovene would be able to recognise himself in the book..." Levstik reveals the deep structure of the sentence as it would be composed before the introduction of the grammatical rule of reflexivity. That rule demands that in a verbal phrase the noun (subject) must be replaced with a personal reflexive pronoun if that noun, as the subject of a subject sentence, depends on the first superimposed knot in the fabric of the sentence: "Narcissus adores Narcissus" – "Narcissus adores himself". This stylistic operation, i.e. the system of meaning "at the second level", sinks its teeth here into the primary system of mother language: it bites it in a way that it reveals something that is otherwise a theoretical construct for the analysis of the primary system of signification (system of meaning). The latter system attaches to the former in a manner that it slips *"under it"*: therefore, the formal structure of that procedure is the same as in a literary-historical commentary – except that literary-historical (-ideological) explanation of Levstik's sentence is a caricature of that procedure as it represents his "farcical" repetition, unless it doesn't know what it really does show. In this way, Levstik's pattern represents the formal-structural paradigm of all its possible interpretations: as much is "its every possible interpretation" an ideologically nationalist (literary-historical) explanation, that much is Levstik's statement a necessary form of discursive practice of nationalism and, at the same time, its necessary object.

As the operation that ideological discourse performs on the discursive sequence (on the statement), that sequence is expressed in the mother language. Given the fact that mother language is nothing other than translatability of a statement into "all" other statements in which that statement is possible to translate into – since the mother language is nothing other than the perpetual possibility of yet another translation – Levstik's sentence, by the virtue of being spoken in mother language, is actually employed in a potential corpus of all statements into which it is translatable into, thus all the statements that can translate it since they regard it as an (ideological) statement articulated in the bosom of the mother language. As a result, Levstik's programmatic sentence is performing its procedure upon all its (possible) (ideological) interpretations that "translate" it (into mother language, in which it must be spoken for them if it should be translatable at all) in such a way that they perform the same operation upon it. Levstik's programme consists of performing that involutive operation upon all possible statements that it is programming, and it is programming them so that they can perform the same procedure on it – a reflexive one and, of course, one that is reflecting or mirroring it. Hence, it is not only that the inner "formal" constitution of the sentence is equivalent to the constitution of relations which that sentence makes with its (ideological) interpretations, but, moreover, that sentence is, according to its *contents*, just an (ideological) interpretation of its own "formal" structure – of linguistic and intertextual structure. Therefore, if our hypothetical ideological interpretation claimed that the sentence is, "according to its contents", people-constitutive, it must now acknowledge that it is people-constitutive also "according to its form" precisely because that form is "aesthetical".

  This hypothetical interpretation has initially offered us the difference between content and form, and then, with the help of it, dissociated the nationalist-ideological element, which it associated with the content, from the aesthetical one, which it associated with the form. If we could then conclude that the "content" of a sentence is just an interpretation of its "form", it is clear that the form must already be ideological, i.e. people-constitutive. Nevertheless, we won't neglect the original hypothesis that enabled such a conclusion, since we must say that the "form" is already in itself people-constitutive precisely because it is aesthetical.

This, of course, is clear even without such a detour through ideological interpretation, since the sentence constitutes a complete imprisonment of the mother language as soon as it encloses itself within it and its interpretations – and as soon as that imprisonment is constituted by the procedure of perpetual mirroring reflection.

This hypothetical explanation has, nonetheless, the "contentual" people-constitutiveness relied upon the fragile self-evidence that the subject and object of literary participation is a member of a nation that speaks the language in which the sentence is constructed, and to which the empirical writer of it belongs to. It may also rely upon it for the ultimate meaning of the statement. We can, of course, appropriate this explanation since the proofing programme precisely determines the strategy of ideological intervention into discursive practice that should interpellate a Slovene into the Slovene. Between a Slovene and the Slovene Levstik is inserting the entire Slovene nation with its centuries-long history. Nevertheless, the other

Slovene, who cannot be grammatically reflected precisely because it represents only a semantic reflex, is an aesthetic figure – not only because s/he is a character in a book and not only because it is the trigger of ideological interpellation that transforms the first wild-grown native into a national subject. There is a much more rudimentary reason for this: that Slovene is written-down in the third person, although it could be in the first person, and, particularly, in the first person of plural. This would indeed represent the way in which a politician speaks – a writer writes in a different way.

The programmatic statement is a literary enclave within the text – and it can become truly programmatic only when it gets separated as a literary statement. A Slovene, for whom thus all that is predetermined, suddenly perceives her/himself in the third person – and it is in the third person that it is visible that s/he is interpellated into a subject through an aesthetical ideological effect. It is only in this way that – from a distance, which is aesthetic – the subject-object can be easily recognised in that double mirroring. If there was some kind of *shifter* employed here – for instance – "us, Slovenes", then it would represent an obvious ideological lure, an empty space where a reader would be invited to place her/himself – but that same reader could understand it also like a vacant place, and thus read the statement in the third person, i.e. as Levstik *et consortes* (and company).

If this possibility is already adopted beforehand by the discourse and actualised by it – then it establishes between the reader and itself the same relationship as the one that it constitutes at the level of statement between the subject and object that remains unreflected precisely because of that. Hence, a Slovene that recognises her/himself in the Slovene (that is being recognised and reflected in a Slovene...) will easily realise that it is her/him that is already inscribed in *that sentence*, that s/he is that Slovene who is looking at *her/himself* in the book. Instead of three subjects (a reader of Levstik's sentence, the reader in Levstik's sentence, and the Slovene from the book) suddenly there are only two – ones that are present in Levstik's formula. From there on, it remains, of course, only one more step to only one Slovene – since it is precisely when the reader *before* the formula will execute reflexivity that is missing *in* the formula. The uneven relation between Slovenians *within* the statement is only an aesthetical representation of the relation between the subject of the statement and the subject of expression: as soon as the native reader with her/his native speaker instincts – occupying the place of the subject of expression – "corrects" the mistake in the statement s/he is already inscribing her/himself in that very statement, inscribing her/himself in the place of a concealed shifter, and therefore within the very sweet-spoken proposed programme. The aesthetical articulation of the content is the condition of its political-programmatic efficacy.

In this way, we could claim, against the ideological explanation, that in Levstik's formula it is the *form* that is people-constitutive and the content aesthetical – with an addendum that such a difference between the content and the form is

only a part of the ideological strategy employed
in that formula.

The same way as we can signify someone
with the name "Turk",[4] behind whom there are
25000 Turks wielding their sabres, we can use
the word "Slovene" to signify only someone that
sees the Slovene in the book. Nevertheless, while
the Christian society is recognised in Quaglio's
frescoes in the Ljubljana cathedral, although the
Romans that persecute the Christians wear turbans –
for ideological interpellation induced from the top of
the cathedral's dome the effect of non-Christianity
is sufficient, which is maybe in its contemporary
political disguise even more efficient as the real
bourgeois ideology wants more for its subjects: a free
personal choice, and it gives more: a free personal
choice. It is, of course, achieved in a way that it
"personally" calls the individual into subjectivity
that is already definitely defined – bourgeois
subjectivity, thus national subjectivity: the literary-
aesthetical interpellation recruits individuals into
Slovenes. Thus, we can say that a Slovene becomes
a member of the nation precisely at the moment
when s/he recognises the Slovene in the book. As
the commitment to become a member of a nation
performs the act upon itself, it is eternally circular,
that programmatic definition of literature enables
and already defines its development into the "real"
aesthetic formation: that Slovene from the book

4   "Fires lick mountain sides, / raising flames up to the sky, / along
       came Turk, raging, killing and torching everything / wherever
       he goes..." Josip Stritar, from the poem *Turki na Slévici* [Turks on
       Slévica] written in the 1860s.

must be visible somewhere and thus it opens the possibility for literature to take itself as its own ideological foundation – and, accordingly, become the "real", as a kind of *l'art-pour-l'art* that moves all the time within its own field thus not having to be borrowed from any political ideologies. In this way, from Levstik to Cankar[5] there is only one step – within the horizon of Levstik's programme. It is, of course, only with that Cankarian step and all that it drags along that Levstik becomes susceptible to analysis that sees "through it". Nevertheless, for literature it is also significant the following: the perpetual circularity of Levstik's formula demands a book within a book, and again a book within that book, etc. Literature in its essayist phase precisely becomes "eternal", meaning the "real" ideology – at least eternal within its own horizon, i.e. as long as it lasts.

5   Ivan Cankar (1876-1918) was a Slovene writer, political activist, playwright, and critic. He is regarded as the greatest Slovene writer and one of the founders of Slovene modernism. At the turn of the century he became openly socialist and joined the Yugoslav Social Democratic Party, while publicly criticising Slovene liberalism and clericalism.

Editorial Statement of
Punk Problemi No. 205/206 (1981)

Editorial: Rastko Močnik, Rado Riha, Miran Božovič, Ervin Hladnik,
Darko Štrajn, Jure Mikuž, Miha Avanzo, Denis Poniž,
Marjan Pungartnik, Drago Bajt, Slavoj Žižek (managing editor).

Dear reader, regarding the issue you are holding in your hands right now, <u>we are well aware that it will probably be seen as a "provocation"</u>. It would be almost superfluous to list the whole range of criticisms that it will probably be subject to: from those that are still "moderate" ("it is true that *even* such texts should be published, but they should be accompanied by an in-depth social-scientific reflection that sheds light on the matter from a broader perspective"; "the texts exude a <u>nihilistic, self-destructive protest</u>, charged with cheap provocations, instead of the youth directing their critical energy in a constructive direction"; "punk is a phenomenon that can be understood from the viewpoint of the disintegration of late capitalist society, but in our country, it can only mean a fashionable intrusion of a foreign ideology"; "punk involves a tiny fraction of the urban youth, but what about the broad masses of those who still retain a sense of a more civilised way of spending their leisure time?; etc., etc.), right down to the infamous *leitmotif* of the bureaucratic manipulator: "So this is the crap our workers' money is being spent on!". We are aware of all of this – and we could go on and on – but still... And yet, I believe that what obliges *Problemi* to publish such an issue is the fact that it is a <u>magazine published by</u> the Republican Conference of the Socialist Youth League of Slovenia, a magazine that is – more than ever

before – supposed to confront the problems of the *actual* cultural life of the "youth" in Slovenia. It is a fact – a fact that is, unfortunately, irrefutably proven by the record sales figures – that punk is indeed a "possible" phenomenon in our country. It is very much "our own" form of "youth" activity, not an "invasion of something foreign"; a phenomenon that, despite all of its "provocativeness", has even received some so-called "social recognition" (the *Sedam sekretara SKOJA* Award for the band *Pankrti*). Of course, a possible answer to this is: true, but these tendencies are precisely the *negative* ones, as punk encompasses all of the issues that the organised forces of youth should be fighting against the hardest (empty nihilism, etc.), <u>punk is a *symptom*</u>... At this point – when it comes to the word "symptom" – I have to admit that I completely agree with the potential critics, although perhaps I ascribe a slightly different dimension to this word: a "symptom" is a phenomenon that at first sight – from the everyday, established perspective – appears as something "alien", as an "intrusion of the immoral". However, what actually intrudes is the otherwise suppressed "truth" of what is apparently the "calmest" and most normal everyday life, which is so outraged and surprised by it. <u>The "symptom" confronts us with our own repressed, displaced truth in a perverted form.</u> Let us recall the "Trobec case" [referring to Metod Trobec,

Editorial Statement of
Punk Problemi No. 205/206 (1981)

a serial killer from Slovenia] that recently stirred up our public, and let us remember the tasteless orgy that the decent "petty-bourgeois" newspapers were engaged in – this is the "truth" about the "normal" everyday life, the truth that punk confronts us with. If the distinction between a non-dogmatic and dogmatic Marxist approach makes any sense, then it lies (also) in the fact that when in the course of investigating social phenomena we encounter a point that has symptomatic value, we should, first of all, *let the "symptom" speak* rather than "interpret" it in advance (i.e., reduce it to what is already known). This is what the present issue seeks to achieve. If someone is "horrified" by it, no big deal. It will only be a problem if someone is "horrified" by it alone, without also questioning themselves and finding out that *de te fabula narratur...* Punk literally *performs* the repressed dimension of the "normal" and, in this way, "liberates" by introducing a certain alienating *distance*. Thus, there is a tendency to emphasise punk's sadomasochism, irrational violence, "anarchism", etc. However, punk establishes distance precisely by staging these elements, by "bringing them out into the open". By no means should we forget that the "explicit" ideology of fascism never entailed the "preaching of irrational violence" but, on the contrary, encouraged the love of one's homeland, making sacrifices for it, and so on... By merely *repeating* a repressed situation and thus "explicating" it – *by making it visible as such –* we trigger a much more powerful

illumination and distancing than by somehow placing it in a "broader perspective" (Kafka, who "merely describes" the fate of the helpless individual, is much more powerful than the "critical realists" in the vein of Thomas Mann). Therefore, dear reader, do not ascribe punk with the position that it has been in fact subverting for years: it is precisely the absence of an "explicit" perspective that suggests that punk is already addressing us from some "utopian", "inalienable" place. Thus, punk as a 'symptom' in a direct existential form encompasses all of what we refer to, in the abstract ideological-political jargon, as "the rule of techno-bureaucratic forces", "the underdevelopment of self-management relations", "the bourgeois and petty-bourgeois ideology that dominates our consumerist everyday life", etc. It is a unique indicator of how the pressure of the techno-bureaucratic forces in the socio-economic sphere intersects with the domination of bourgeois ideological forms in (mass) culture. That is why – if I may conclude this contribution with a "provocation" as well – I stand behind this issue not only as the "managing editor", but also and above all as a member of the League of Communists, as a communist – a worker in the field of culture and theory.

– Managing editor

Editorial Statement of
Punk Problemi No. 221 (1982)

Editorial: Miha Avanzo, Miran Božovič, Mladen Dolar (managing editor), Branko Gradišnik, Milan Jesih, Miha Kovač, Peter Mlakar, Rastko Močnik, Denis Poniž, Rado Riha, Jože Vogrinc, Zdenko Vrdlovec.

When the first punk issue of the *Problemi* magazine was published a year and a half ago, its cover stated that punk was a **symptom**, and symptoms, as we know from psychoanalytic theory, reoccur in the same place. Thus, punk, persisting as a symptom that is so much more pressing insofar as it remains a foreign element in "our culture", reoccurs in *Problemi* – in the only place left for it in the Slovenian newspaper and magazine arena. In the time that has passed since the first issue dedicated to punk, we have witnessed plenty of drastic and exaggerated campaigns against it in the public media, which ultimately turned into nothing short of generalised, anti-youth chauvinism based on a few marginalities tailored to sensationalism. The editorial of the *Problemi* magazine has therefore decided to avoid two of the most frequent ideological moves:
– understanding and reducing punk to either completely negative, or even positive formulas or mottos already in advance, thus avoiding facing it while employing it in the context of a pre-planned ideological project, most often as a means of intimidation;
– preliminary separation of a good and a bad punk, where the good variety is supposed to be cherished and supported, while the bad one should be suppressed. As if by coincidence, it then always happens that the unpleasant, critical aspects of punk are proclaimed as just a few isolated, extreme examples and thus separated from the majority and the supposedly "healthy core".

Quite the opposite, the goal of the present issue is to let punk speak, as it is still often violently silenced, as well as to show a broad enough range of the various orientations within punk itself that cannot merely be reduced to a single common denominator, and that range as far as the very problematic sympathies for anarchism, which should be articulated and consolidated rather than left floating in an intangible and semi-forbidden sphere of drawing on the walls. We are convinced that this is the only path towards a democratic discussion and a critical confrontation with punk, whose mass appeal and popularity can certainly not be questioned. Naturally, this path involves the risk of swift disqualifications, hypocritical indignation, and emotionally-charged outbursts; yet we trust in the power of democratic and rational discussion.

Naturally, the editors are well aware that the current issue may stir up a variety of adverse reactions and give rise to severely unfavourable standpoints. However, we are adamant in our conviction that the other alternative – to continue to silence punk, attempt to stifle it with harsh repression or pretend that it does not exist – would eventually lead to much more damaging social consequences.

– Managing editor